HOLY
CURRENCIES

Other Books by Eric H.F. Law

The Wolf Shall Dwell with the Lamb:
A Spirituality for Leadership in a Multicultural Community

The Bush Was Blazing but Not Consumed

Inclusion: Making Room for Grace

Sacred Acts, Holy Change:
Faithful Diversity and Practical Transformation

Finding Intimacy in a World of Fear

HOLY
CURRENCIES

6 Blessings for Sustainable Missional Ministries

by Eric H.F. Law

CHALICE
PRESS

ST. LOUIS, MISSOURI

Bible quotations, unless otherwise marked, are from the *New Revised Standard Version Bible,* copyright 1989, Division of Christian Education of the National Council of the Churches of Christ in the United States of America. Used by permission. All rights reserved.

Scripture quotations marked NIV are taken from the HOLY BIBLE, NEW INTERNATIONAL VERSION®. NIV®. Copyright © 1973, 1978, 1984 by International Bible Society. Used by permission of Zondervan Publishing House. All rights reserved.

Cover image: File licensed by www.depositphotos.com/daksel
Cover design: Scribe Inc.
Interior design: Hui-Chu Wang

www.chalicepress.com

Print: 9780827214927   EPUB: 9780827214934   EPDF: 9780827214941

Library of Congress Cataloging-in-Publication Data

Law, Eric H. F.
Holy currencies : six blessings for sustainable missional ministries /
by Eric H.F. Law.
pages cm
ISBN 978-0-8272-1492-7 — ISBN 978-0-8272-1494-1 — ISBN 978-0-8272-1493-4
1. Missions--Study and teaching. I. Title.
BV2090.L27 2013
253—dc23   2012047652

Printed in the United States of America

Dedications:

In memory of my mother, Law Tam Un-Oi, who taught me to live the Cycle of Blessings from the day I was born.

For Ellio Chiho Law, my godson and grandnephew, and Claire Miranda Dawes, my grandniece; may you continue the blessings that flow from your great-grandmother.

Contents

Acknowledgments

The year 2012 has been an extremely busy one, and finding time to write this book has been challenging. Many ideas in this book emerged from the weekly discipline of writing for my blog: The Sustainist-Spirituality for Sustainable Communities in a Networked World. I want to thank my loyal readers for their encouragements and feedback.

My journey to accessing *Holy Currencies* in concrete and conscious ways began with the founding of the Kaleidoscope Institute in 2006. I am extremely grateful to Bishop Jon Bruno, who said yes to this entrepreneurial ministry idea and Bishop Chet Talton who accepted the invitation to be the first president of the board of directors. Subsequently, I give thanks to Bishop Diane Jardine Bruce, the second president of the board, who has been a fervent advocate, sharing her currency of relationship in support of the Institute.

I am grateful to colleagues who consistently gave me feedback on the Holy Currencies in the last two years: Lucky Lynch, Bill Cruse, Mark Smutny, Leroy Chambliss, Stacy Kitahata, Kristina Gonzalez, Marcia Patton, Patricia Millard, Denise Trevino, Linda Young, Dan Valdez, Anita Hendrix, Nedi Rivera, Randy Stearns, Bill Stanley, Michael Cunningham, and Deborah Dunn. I thank Mimi Grant and Bob Kelley for being promoters and supporters of Holy Currencies and for challenging me to take these ideas further out into the world.

I especially want to thank the individuals and church teams that came to the Holy Currencies workshops in the last years— the sixteen church teams from the Episcopal Diocese of Pennsylvania, the good people from the Riverside Presbytery, the leaders of the Episcopal Diocese of Eastern Oregon, the participants of the first Holy Currencies training in Trinity Conference Center in Connecticut, and the participants of the Winter and Summer Kaleidoscope Institutes in Los Angeles.

I am appreciative of Desiree Glover, the Kaleidoscope Institute administrator, for keeping the institute running while I was preoccupied in writing this book. I thank Kent Steinbrenner and Bill Cruse for their insightful feedbacks and proofreading skill. I especially want to thank

Kent Steinbrenner for designing the Holy Currencies and Cycle of Blessings graphic used in this book and in all my workshop promotional materials. I am grateful to Steve Rutberg for his understanding during the stressful time when I struggled to write this book last year.

Finally, as we come upon the twentieth anniversary of the publication of my first book, *The Wolf Shall Dwell with the Lamb*, I want to give thanks to Chalice Press for this long, mutually respectful, and beneficial relationship and especially for having faith in my work from the beginning.

Introduction

During the 2009 Convention of the Episcopal Diocese of Los Angeles, I surveyed thirty-seven congregations. Over half of the congregations struggled with concerns around money. The U.S. economy in previous years obviously had negatively impacted local churches, which depend primarily on giving from members. Also, over the previous two years, the speakers at diocesan conventions and clergy conferences all focused on "missional ministry," "Emergent Church" and "Fresh Expressions."[1] It is no accident that over half of the church leaders surveyed also expressed concerns about how they could move their churches toward becoming missional. The result of the survey started me on a journey in search of resources to empower local churches to become both sustainable and missional.

A missional church is a community of people who look outward and are able to connect with others who are not already members of any church organization. Reggie McNeal, in his book *Missional Renaissance*, described three shifts that need to happen for churches to be missional.

1. *From an internal to an external focus*
2. *From program development to people development*
3. *From church-based to kingdom-based leadership*[2]

The Emergent or Emerging Church movement in the United States and Fresh Expressions in the U.K. and New Zealand both advocate for a church to be more relational, authentic, and able to share authority in order to reach the so-called emerging generation. Based on my research and learning from these resources, I had already designed a program called "Missional Ministry in the Grace Margin," which engages local congregation members in faithful conversation, fostering missional thinking and actions. So I was confident that I could provide resources in the missional part of this exploration.

However, when it comes to money, I was at a loss. If I were to find or create resources that assist our local congregations to address

---

[1]Brian McClaren and Phyllis Tickle spoke to us about Emergent Church, and Archbishop David Moxon of New Zealand shared the Fresh Expression Movements in the U.K. and New Zealand.
[2]Reggie McNeal, *Missional Renaissance* (San Francisco: Jossey-Bass, a Wiley Imprint, 2009), 6–17.

money issues, where would I begin? I am not an economist. I am not an accountant. I am not a businessman. I am not a stewardship officer of any church. What authority do I have to even begin to address concerns between money and church?

After I got over my sense of inadequacy on this whole topic, I was determined to begin like I always begin any ministry project—by listening. So, I listened to the good folks of our church communities in different denominations, and consistently I heard the word "sustainability." "How can we make our ministry sustainable?" The issues or problems were described variously as, "Where do we find the money to finance our ministries?" or, "How can we raise the money to start a needed ministry?" The worst situations had to do with closing of an existing ministry or letting go of personnel because of the lack of funds. Obviously, these expressions were not that of a missional church. I discovered that people who spoke about being missional tended not to talk about sustainability, and those who spoke about sustainability, often focusing on money as the only currency, tended not to talk about being missional.

Upon further reflection on the money issues that our churches were facing, I realized I did know something about money and sustainable ministry. In 2006, I started the Kaleidoscope Institute as a separate 501(c)3 organization associated with the Episcopal Diocese of Los Angeles. With the shrinking budget of the diocese, I knew a number of diocesan staff, of which I was a part, would have to be let go. I went to my bishop and proposed the formation of the Kaleidoscope Institute using the modest amount of leftover budgeted funds from my old job as seed money. In four years, as the U.S. economy continued to struggle, and when the budgets of many churches—local and national, in all the denominations—continued to diminish, the Kaleidoscope Institute flourished. We have increased our annual budget by 700 percent. We even did it without doing fundraising for the first three years. Our income came almost entirely from contributions given by individuals and church organizations in exchange for the leadership-training programs and resources that we provided.

What made the Kaleidoscope Institute sustainable was not just about the money. We were serving, resourcing and building networks of relationships with many leaders and organizations, not only in the Episcopal Church, but also in all the major Christian denominations and civic communities. Through these relationships, we discovered what their needs and interests were, and provided relevant training and resources for them so that they could increase their ability to connect with diverse populations and increase their congregational vitality. I began to look beyond money as the only currency for sustainability. As I studied other ministries that I considered to be missional *and* sustainable, I noticed again that money was not the only currency at work. After more than a year of research, I concluded that there are at least five other currencies that flow through a sustainable missional ministry. In addition to money, these currencies are time and place, gracious leadership, relationship, truth and wellness. From the beginning, the Kaleidoscope Institute was sustainable because it utilized all six currencies. These currencies "flow" through the ministry, exchanging themselves for other currencies, forming what I called the "Cycle of Blessings." The sequence of exchanges rejuvenates that which was spent initially, recirculating resources, and regenerating more currencies, thereby growing and expanding the ministry. Here is how the Cycle of Blessings works for the Kaleidoscope Institute.

Time and Place: One of the principal ministries of the Kaleidoscope Institute involves the training institutes we offer in different parts of the U.S. and Canada. In order to provide these institutes, we reserve a "place," such as a retreat or conference center, to house the participants. The Institute also needs to contract our associates and facilitators to commit the "time" to deliver the training.

Gracious Leadership: In exchange for the participants' investment of their "money" and "time" to attend the institute, they receive training and resources to develop their "gracious leadership"; they learn how to develop skills, tools, models and processes to create gracious environment (Grace Margin) within which meaningful equitable "relationships" across different cultures can be built. The different cultures can be related to race and ethnicity. age, gender, sexual orientation, class, or simply those between church members and other folks in the neighborhood.

Relationship: After the training, participants return to their churches and ministries, using the skills they learned to strengthen existing "relationships" within their organizations. They also utilize their "gracious leadership" skills to enable members to extend themselves outward to build "relationships" with people of different cultural backgrounds, especially in their neighborhood.

Truth: As they get to know more people in the community through these relationships, they might discover the "truth" of the different people's experiences living in their community. The truth might be gifts that need to be lifted up and celebrated, naming the injustice and oppression against certain populations, or discovering their own lack of spiritual wellness.

Wellness: Kindled by the "truth," they might mobilize their currencies of time and place, leadership and relationship to assist individuals and communities to achieve "wellness." This "wellness" can include physical, spiritual, social, ecological or financial aspects.

Money: Realizing how they benefited from the "gracious leadership" that nurtured and supported their "wellness," many communities decide to commit "money" and "time" for additional leaders to attend future training institutes provided by the Kaleidoscope Institute. Sometimes they covenant with the Institute for our associates and facilitators to come and provide training on-site. The "money" they contribute to the Institute then goes to support our staff "time" and to reserve a "place" to provide the "gracious leadership" training for more leaders. And the Cycle of Blessings starts over again.

Even though I have described the Cycle of Blessings as it applies to the Kaleidoscope Institute, in the order as it is laid out in the Holy Currencies diagram, the flowing of these currencies does not necessarily moves in the same order for other sustainable ministries. For example, for another ministry, we might begin with relationships, which might flow into money, which then exchanges for time and place, where gracious leadership provides resources to achieve wellness, which then helps people speak the truth, which might then lead to more relationships. There are, of course, many other combinations. We will explore each one of these currencies in detail through the chapters of this book.

Chapters 3, 5, 7, 9, 11 and 13 explore in full the six currencies that make up the Cycle of Blessing. Each of these chapters answers the following questions for each currency:

• What is this currency?
• How can this currency be developed?
• For what can this currency be exchanged?
• How do we value and measure this currency in our ministry?

Each of these chapters provides suggested exercises and activities for individuals and groups to explore and understand this currency. There are also processes and exercises for churches to do an inventory of their current use of this currency, to develop this currency and to enable their church members to measure and value this currency.

In-between these chapters, I tell stories of different sustainable missional ministries, both in the church and in secular settings. These stories, from my research and readings, hopefully will push you to think beyond your church's boundaries as you explore these different currencies and how you can access and flow these Holy Currencies, thereby making both your church missional and the wider community more sustainable.

So come, explore, and enter the Cycle of Blessings with me.

CHAPTER ONE

Praise God from Whom All Blessings Flow

The earth is the Lord's and all that is in it,
    the world, and those who live in it;
for he has founded it on the seas,
    and established it on the rivers. *(Psalm 24:1–2)*

Everything belongs to God because God created everything (Colossians 1:16), including money (Haggai 2:8). God renews and recreates the earth so that there is an abundance of resources for all to share and enjoy. Since we do not own anything, we are not to keep anything.

When you send forth your spirit, they are created,
    and you renew the face of the ground. *(Psalm 104:30)*

In God's creation, everything gets recycled, including that which we consider to be waste. From biology class, I learned that the oxygen we breathe into our lungs is used to refresh our blood; in exchange, we breathe out carbon dioxide, which plants and other green organisms take in, working with the earth's sun and water through a process of photosynthesis, creating not only food but releasing oxygen for us and other creatures to breathe in. Our roles as children of God are to be part the recirculation of resources so that all living things on earth may share God's abundance.

As the rain and the snow come down from heaven, and do not return to it without watering the earth and making it bud and flourish, so that it yields seed for the sower and bread for the eater, so is my word that goes out from my mouth: It will not return to me empty, but will accomplish what I desire and achieve the purpose for which I sent it. *(Isaiah 55:10–11, NIV)*

In this text from Isaiah, God further instructs us to learn from nature's recycling ways, applying them to human relationships and creating sustainable communities. We are to receive God's word like water. As God's word works through our lives, our communities, and our nations, it enables growth, rejuvenates communities, and then is recycled again. Even with God's word, we do not own it but must recirculate it, again and again offering blessings to all who receive it.

When they were satisfied, he told his disciples, "Gather up the fragments left over, so that nothing may be lost." *(John 6:12)*

On these fundamental assumptions we begin our exploration of the Cycle of Blessings:

1. God owns everything.
2. God gives abundantly.
3. We are not to keep God's resources; we are to circulate these resources.
4. God's blessings are then recycled to create more blessings.

Currencies Must Flow

My family was considered poor by the monetary-minded world, but I did not know it. We did not have much money, because as far back as I can remember, money was coming in and going out, and coming in and going out again. However, in the process, no one was hungry. There was also a job for anyone who wanted to work and be part of the currency of money that moved through the family business. I do not want to paint a completely rosy picture, because there were times when I knew my mother was strapped for money, but, just as the stories often told to us, something always worked out, often in the form of "sisters"—my mother's trusted friends—coming through with some money to help us. My mother once explained to me about our family business this way: "We don't make a lot of money. But everyone who works in the business gets a piece of it." My childhood experience, being formed by my mother's way of managing currencies in her personal life, family and business, implanted a fundamental perspective I have had about money and other currencies that might have played a part in the success and sustainability of the Kaleidoscope Institute many years later. That is, I have always thought of currency as something that moves.

My parents started a music school in Hong Kong in the 1960s, which has continued until today in New York City with the same business model—a sustainable business that never makes much money, but certainly has made a lot of friends and provided livelihood for many people over the years—people such as music teachers who were like my parents' daughters and sons, workers who were like brothers or sisters to us growing up, and students who had grown up and brought their children to take music lessons at our music school. When I visit the music school in New York, I often hear parents of students talking about how they were students at my parents' music school in Hong Kong. In the last fifteen years, I have been involved in the management of the music school in New York and, indeed, the company has not made much money. But it is the movement of the money, the "currency," that has kept the business going—providing jobs, learning, and enrichment for thousands of people over the years. Here is how it works:

My father was a furniture maker. He got in the business of assembling pianos, focusing on the carpentry work. My mother noticed that it was very expensive for a child to learn to play the piano—the family had to buy a piano and pay for private lessons. She also noticed that children did not have a lot of places to go after school. She further noticed that parents who worked could use a few more hours each week to do what they needed to do to support their families. What she noticed was the truth that drove the ministry's need. With my father's construction and carpentry skills, we built a number of soundproofed rooms in our apartment, put a piano in each room, and hired teachers to offer lessons. We charged the parents a modest amount each month; in exchange, the students received one half-hour lesson a week and could come to practice five days a week. The fee collected would be shared equally with the teachers—50 percent for the teacher, and 50 percent for the school to support the staff who administered, maintained, and coordinated the students and scheduling. Follow the flow of currencies and you will discover why this business model has been sustainable for over fifty years. The modest amount of money that the parents paid flowed into supporting a "time and place" for their children to learn. The arrangement also exchanged the modest amount for a few extra hours in the week that the parents could use to provide for their family, knowing their children were safe. This money further flowed into providing an income for the teachers in exchange for their "leadership" and expertise in this art. The currency continued to flow in providing jobs for others—the piano tuners, the cousin who lived with and worked for us in exchange for doing the maintenance of the rooms. The company never made any money because money did not stay; it kept moving. It flowed in constructive directions, providing blessings for many: the learning of an art, safety, extra time to build wellness of individuals and family, etc.

I grew up with a Chinese saying, "Water is money." I often heard it as a joke, especially when it was raining—all the rain became a wish or a symbol of financial abundance. In spoken Cantonese, I also heard people use the word for "water" in place of money. Perhaps we should think of the currency of money or any other currency as being like water—it should move and flow. In the summer, I make sure that there are no pools of stagnant water around the house, because they will be a breeding environment for mosquitoes and other insects that are carriers of diseases. When water does not flow, it creates opportunities for destructive things to grow. In other words, it rots. I would say the same thing goes for money and resources: when they are not flowing, or when we hold on to them, they turn rotten and become breeding pools for trouble and unsustainability.

There was the same amount of money in existence before and after the 2009 financial crisis in the United States. Where did the money go? Some people in the financial "industry" had been reaping benefits from inflated financial transactions for years, but instead of recirculating the money back into the system—especially back to investors—they held on to it and stopped the flow. It then turned rotten and is stinking up the whole country.

> Some give freely, yet grow all the richer;
> others withhold what is due, and only suffer want.
> *(Proverb 11:24)*

Blessing or Curse—Our Choice

In 2010, we witnessed not only the stagnation of money in the United States, but also the use of money in exchange for destructive and divisive causes. For example, in the November 2010 election, Meg Whitman, a candidate for governor of California, reportedly spent $144 million on her campaign. Living in California, I remember being bombarded by negative ads over and over again on all the major TV channels. We are talking about $144 million, all going to buy time on TV for negative, divisive ads! Imagine what we could do with $144 million for constructive, life-giving, relationship-building, truth-telling, and leadership-developing efforts! How about helping 1440 families to keep their homes, supporting 144 California schools, empowering 144 sustainable communities, creating 14,400 jobs, or forming job-training programs for 14,400 people! I am sure if Ms.

Whitman had done any of these constructive things with her money, she would have gotten the votes she needed to become the next governor of California!

So, we have a choice in what we do with the resources over which we have control. We can choose to hold on to them and let them turn rotten, or use them to further divisive and destructive causes; *or*, we can choose to let them flow in life-giving, truth-telling, relationship-building, community-enhancing ways.

I call heaven and earth to witness against you today that I have set before you life and death, blessings and curses. Choose life, so that you and your descendants may live. *(Deuteronomy 30:19)*

From Money to Blessing

Recall an earlier time in your life when money was flowing in a way that gives blessings. It could be a story or experience in which your parents, relatives, friends, or elders had used money in a way that built relationships, told the truth, fostered wellness, or built up the community.

- Where were you?
- Who was there?
- What were you doing?
- Where did the money involved come from?
- What blessings did the money exchange for?
- Who or what group was enriched?
- What long-term benefits did this create?

How did this experience impact the way you use money today...

...personally?

...for your ministry?

Currency Redefined

The word *currency* comes from the Medieval Latin word *currentia*, which literally means "a flowing," and from the Latin word *currere*, which means "to run or flow." It was John Locke in 1699 who first used the word *currency* to refer to circulation of money.[1] Since then, the word *currency* in the English language has been used most often as referring to money.

Merriam-Webster.com defines *currency* as "something that is in circulation as a medium of exchange." I would like to ride on the word

---

[1]Available at: Online Etymology Dictionary at: http://www.etymonline. com

something in this definition and explore the concept of currency beyond just money. From the example of my family business to the formation of the Kaleidoscope Institute, there were certainly other currencies besides money that were in circulation as mediums of exchange, which made these ministries sustainable. When I researched different sustainable ministries and how they functioned, the key question was: "What other currencies are flowing through this ministry?" As I learned more and more about what made these ministries sustainable and missional, several currencies—mediums of exchange—kept surfacing as keys to their successes. They are (as mentioned in the Introduction):

- Time and Place
- Gracious Leadership
- Relationship
- Truth
- Wellness
- Money

These are not the only currencies, for others are at work in many sustainable and missional ministries. I am simply pointing out, from my research and observation, that these are the essential ones that a sustainable and missional ministry must have circulating through its operation, interacting not only within the membership of the organization but also with the wider environment and community.

Definitions of the Six Currencies for the Cycle of Blessings

Currency of Time and Place: Paid and volunteer time that leaders and members offer to the church or ministry. Properties from which a church and ministry operates, and other properties owned or which can be accessed by the church and ministry.

Currency of Gracious Leadership: The ability to use skills, tools, models, and processes to create gracious environments (Grace Margin) within which mutually respectful "relationships" and the discernment of the "truth" across differences can be built internally, among existing members, and externally, with non-members. Differences can be racial/ethnic, age, gender, sexual orientation, class, political affiliation, or simply those existing between church members and other folks in the neighborhood.

Currency of Relationship: The internal and external networks of mutually respectful connections that leaders and members of a church and ministry have. Internal connections include constructive relationships among members and leaders, area churches or ministries of the same affiliation, area denominational organizations, and national and international denominational structures. External connections include constructive relationships with non-members, different racial, cultural and ethnic groups in the neighborhood, people with resources and people in need in the community, civic community leaders, ecumenical and interfaith partners, community and civic organizations, and local businesses.

Currency of Truth: The ability to articulate individually and corporately the global and wholistic truth, both internally—the experiences of different individuals and groups within the church or ministry—and externally—the experiences of different individuals and groups in the community, the neighborhood, the city or town, the nation, and the earth.

Currency of Wellness: The state of being healthy physically, socially, economically, ecologically, and spiritually within a church or ministry, the neighborhood, the town and city, nation, or the earth, especially as the result of deliberate effort. Sustainable wellness requires regenerative and circulatory flow of material, human, financial, and natural resources.

Currency of Money: Something generally accepted as a medium of exchange, a measure of value, or as a means of payment.

I want to reiterate three points. First, it is the *flowing* of these currencies that gives them value. The dynamic exchanges of these currencies are what circulate and regenerate resources, making a ministry sustainable and missional. For example, a church might have a beautiful church building—a currency of place. But if it is only used on Sunday when the church members come to worship, the currencies of time and place are not being maximized, because it only flows into the currencies of leadership, internal relationship, and wellness one day a week. For the rest of week, this currency of place has no value. And, if a currency does not flow, it has no value.

Second, the flowing of the currencies needs to include all six currencies in order for the ministry to be sustainable and missional. For example, if a church uses the time of volunteers and paid staff to provide wellness to their members only, members are then expected to provide the money needed to maintain the place—the building— and continue to pay the staff. This church, using only three of the six currencies, is not going to be sustainable. It is certainly not missional, with no energy and resources flowing outward in building external relationships. We are witnessing many churches running into financial trouble precisely because of this lack of awareness of other essential currencies. For a church ministry to be sustainable and missional, the currencies of time and place and leadership must be devoted to relationship-building outside the existing membership, and only by doing so will the church be able to listen to and advocate for the truth in the wider community. Developing these two currencies— relationship and truth—externally will ultimately assist the wider community in which the church resides to achieve wellness, making the church's ministries missional. When the community is well, people will contribute money to support the continuing church ministry, making the church financially sustainable.

Third, the flowing of these currencies must recirculate back to replenish what was spent, so that the ministry can be regenerative. In most cases, when the Cycle of Blessings is spinning in a ministry, it not only replenishes the initial investment of the various currencies, it also increases them—and I am not just talking about money. For example, the Kaleidoscope Institute had grown financially by 700 percent in four years. But in terms of time and place, we went from providing one training institute in 2006 in Los Angeles to providing four institutes in 2010 in different parts of the U.S. and Canada. In terms of gracious leadership, we went from one associate—me—to nine associates and at least twenty facilitators. In terms of relationships, as of 2012, we have over 200 graduates of our basic training and at least 2,000 who read our newsletter, *Grace Margin*. We have ongoing relationships with four seminaries, and with leaders from all the major church denominations, both locally and nationally. In terms of truth, through our newsletters, training programs, and resourcing ministries, associates and facilitators of the Institute continue to speak about the injustice that occurs in multicultural environments and the need for inter-culturally competent leaders. In terms of wellness, we consistently receive feedback from our graduates reporting how the skills and tools they learned from our training and resources have helped them create inclusive, sustainable communities.

The Cycle of Blessings is the dynamic exchanges of these six currencies, flowing inward to renew and strengthen internal relationships and increase gracious leadership capacity, and flowing outward to connect, discern the truth, and foster wellness in the wider community. Learning how to develop, access, and "flow" these currencies are essential skills that members of the church must have in order for the church to be sustainable and missional.

Praise God from whom all blessings flow
Circling through earth so all may grow
Vanquishing fear so all may give
Widening grace so all may live

CHAPTER TWO

Do More with Less

When I was a child, my family always had guests for dinner. On any given day, there might be twelve to fifteen people at the dinner table. Dinner was a time of joyful sharing of food and stories. I thought we were quite wealthy, feeding so many people every night. Only when I was older, while talking to my mother about the good old days, did I find out that we were not rich at all. My mother told me that some days she only had three dollars to feed fifteen people. How could that be? I could not remember a day when there was not enough food!

What my mother did with three dollars was a miracle in itself. If you asked her how she did it, she would tell you how she determined what to buy in what season and, more importantly, her techniques in bargaining. But I think there is more to this miracle than just knowing what to buy and how to bargain. Not only was everyone around the table filled every night; there were always leftovers. I believe the way we dealt with the leftovers at the dinner table is indicative of how this miracle of doing "more with less" was accomplished.

Toward the end of dinner, there was always something left on a plate in the middle of the table. Everyone would be staring at it, especially when it was a piece of meat, which was an occasional, special treat. But no one would make a move to take it. Then someone would say, "Why don't you take it, Grandma? You are the oldest." But my grandma would say, "No, I've been eating this stuff all my life. Give it to the little one. He's the youngest and needs the nourishment to grow up to be big and strong." Now all eyes were on me, who was the youngest. But I, who also learned this ritual, would say, "No, not me. I am completely full because I have the smallest stomach. Give it to my older brother. He has an examination at school tomorrow. He needs it so he can do well." My oldest brother would say, "No, not me. Give it to my sister. She has a piano lesson tomorrow..." The ritual would go on around the table; each person would find an excuse not to take the leftover piece of food. While we offered it to each other, we also affirmed each other's worthiness in the family. As a result, the piece of meat would sit in the middle of the table, destined to be left over, to be transformed into a new delicious dish the next day. The leftovers became a symbol of our appreciation of each other's worth. This leftover piece of food became a sign of the abundance we shared—we can do more with less.[1]

At the dinner table of my childhood, I learned a very important life lesson, which has become part of the spirituality I strive to live out in all of my life. The lesson was very different from a more popular spirituality based on scarcity, which drives us to take and keep and to have more than the other. If our goal in life is to take resources and keep them, then everything is stationary; there is not any movement, nor any dynamic exchanges. The spirituality I learned at my dinner table begins with the assumption that there is enough and therefore it is okay to have less than the other. By insisting on having less than the other—"No, not me; let someone else have this"—we kept the blessing flowing in the form of the affirmation of each other's worth. The dynamics of passing the "leftover" around, generating a spirit of appreciation and affirmation, did so much more than fighting over the last piece of meat, as a fear-of-scarcity-minded group would do.

Jesus consistently taught his followers to practice this spirituality of abundance. Here are some of his sayings that many will find incomprehensible unless they live this spirituality.

- "And if anyone wants to sue you and take your coat, give your cloak as well; and if anyone forces you to go one mile, go also the second mile. Give to everyone who begs from you, and do not refuse from anyone who wants to borrow from you." *(Matthew 5:40–42)*
- "No one has greater love than this, to lay down one's life for one's friends." *(John 15:13)*

Jesus' followers, even his closest friends, did not understand what he was talking about. Is it not foolish to give until you have less, and, in Jesus' proposal, give until you have nothing? When Jesus suffered and died on the cross on Good Friday, it confirmed their greatest fear—

---

[1] I first told this story of my childhood diner table in Eric H. F. Law, *Inclusion* (St. Louis: Chalice Press, 2000), 32–33.

when one gives everything away, one dies. This fear was the greatest stumbling block for them to understand Jesus' message.

> For the message about the cross is foolishness to those who are perishing, but to us who are being saved it is the power of God... For God's foolishness is wiser than human wisdom, and God's weakness is stronger than human strength. *(1 Corinthians 1: 18, 25)*

Then came Easter, and the Resurrection, and death was not the end but the beginning. The cross—to give until one has nothing, which was foolishness and unsustainable to the world—became the cornerstone of a new kind of sustainable community. Jesus's followers finally understood what Jesus was showing them. All the miracles that Jesus performed—feeding the multitudes, healing the sick, and releasing the captives—were simply part of this spirituality of abundance. The dynamics created by giving until one has less became an endless circulating of resources, like water working through the earth, rejuvenating lives and regenerating nurturing communities. Suddenly, "do more with less" made sense and was doable. Easter unblocked and released a flood of blessings through Jesus' followers, and, with great joy and passion, they formed the first Christian communities—missional and sustainable.

> All who believed were together and had all things in common; they would sell their possessions and goods and distribute the proceeds to all, as any had need. *(Acts 2:44–45)*

In order to practice this spirituality, people in our communities must believe in the abundance that comes from giving. If everyone in our community gives until he or she has less, it will generate a dynamic that will keep everyone giving and receiving. Eventually what we give away will actually return to us in new forms with new gifts. Once we realize that giving is not a one-time "losing" game, but part of a dynamic process that keeps resources flowing in our community, we will have the courage to give generously.

A Do-More-with-Less Experience

To demonstrate how this works, here is an exercise you can do with any group in your communities to show how "do more with less" can work.

Material needed: 100 notecards.
Size of group: 8–25 participants.

Instructions:

1. Divide the notecards into two piles of 50 cards.
2. Give two participants 50 cards each. Explain that each card represents a kind of currency. It could be money, time, talent, relationship, etc.
3. Explain the rules of this simulation as follows: *The two participants who have the cards are rich with resources. If we live the spirituality of scarcity, most of us would want to keep what we have. In that case, nothing will happen—no movement, no flow of currencies. The two resource-rich persons might decide to trade with each other, but there will be no engagement with those who have nothing. What if the new rule for this community is: It is better to have less than the other? What would happen? Can you imagine that? For the two of you who have, as you encounter another who has none, what would you do with this new spirituality? The one with 50 cards would give at least 26 cards away to another participant who has none. Let's try that. Now if everyone in this community is committed to live out this new spirituality, what will happen?*
4. Give the group time to experience this. Observe what happens. The cards will be distributed to everyone in the room. Those who gave away their cards initially will eventually and very quickly get some cards back, particularly if they have given everything away. The process will evolve into an endless dynamic of giving and receiving. This is what doing more with less looks like.
5. After some time, stop the simulation and invite participants to complete the sentences:
   I noticed...
   I wonder...
6. After participants have shared what they noticed and wondered about, engage them in a conversation on stewardship. Invite participants to imagine the cards in this exercise as other kinds of currency in addition to money—such as time, talent, relationship, leadership, etc. Explore the question: What does this exercise teaches us about sustainability?

"Whoever believes in me...streams of living water will flow from within [them]." *(John 7:38, NIV)*

CHAPTER THREE

Currency of Relationship

Most of us have heard of "six degrees of separation," which refers to the idea that everyone is on average approximately six relationships away from any other person on earth. This means I can make a chain of "a-friend-of-a-friend" statements that connect me with any other person in this world in six steps or fewer. This theory was originally set out by Frigyes Karinthy and popularized in a play written by John Guare[1].

Three Degrees of Influences

Not so well known is the theory of "three degrees of influence" by Nicholas A. Christakis and James H. Fowler. According to this theory, "Everything we do or say tends to ripple through our network, having an impact on our friends (one degree), our friends' friends (two degrees), and even our friends' friends' friends (three degrees). Our influence gradually dissipates and ceases to have a noticeable effect on people beyond the social frontier that lies at three degrees of separation."[2] This means if I am happy, my friends are more likely to be happy, and my friends' friends are more likely to be happy, and my friends' friends' friends are also more likely to be happy. Sadly, if I am suicidal, my friends' friends' friends are more likely to be suicidal. Whether we know it or not, our network of relationships can spread goodness and blessing, or destructiveness and curses.

---

[1]Frigyes Karinthy proposed the theory in his 1929 short story "Chains," popularized in the play "Six Degrees of Separation" by John Guare.

[2]See Nicholas A. Christakis and James H Fowler, *Connected* (New York: Back Bay Books/Little, Brown and Company, 2009), 26–30.

Christakis and Fowler wrote:
Social networks have value precisely because they help us to achieve what we could not achieve on our own...networks influence the spread of joy, the search for sexual partners, the maintenance of health, the functioning of markets, and the struggle for democracy. Yet, social-network effects are not always positive. Depression, obesity, sexually transmitted diseases, financial panic, violence, and even suicide also spread. Social networks, it turns out, tend to magnify whatever they are seeded with.[3]

Through their research on social networks, Christakis and Fowler describe the "Rules of Life in the Network" as follows:

1. We shape our network.
2. Our network shapes us.
3. Our friends affect us.
4. Our friends' friends' friends affect us.
5. The network has a life of its own.[4]

While I know that my social network shapes me, I also know that I can shape my network by influencing my friends, who in turn can influence their friends, and so on. We have a choice in choosing who is in our network or which network we are part of. We also have a choice to decide what to spread through our network. Do we use it to spread lies or tell truth, instill fear or foster trust, propagate hate or share love, control or empower, break down or build sustainable communities? Christakis and Fowler remind us, "[O]ur interconnection is not only a natural and necessary part of our lives but also a force for good."[5]

An inspiring worship at a church that moves 100 participants to do good in the community can have the potential of influencing (if each person in the network has at least five friends) 500 people in the first degree, 2,500 people in the second degree and 12,500 people in the third degree to also do good. In a small town of under 10,000 people, this means what happens in worship for a small church can have the potential to influence almost everybody in the community. We have great responsibility, then, for the networks of which we are a part. As a Christian, I am a part of one of the largest faith networks in the world. I need to value my role in this network and do my part in

---

[3]Ibid., 30–31.
[4]Ibid., 16–36.
[5]Ibid., xvi.

calling the people in my network back to following Jesus, who seeded this network with grace and truth.

Danger of Disconnect

Two thousand years ago, Jesus initiated a network of followers who were charged to be his witnesses, first locally (in Jerusalem), and then to nearby towns and communities (Samaria), and to "the ends of the earth." It was a daunting task, but in view of what we now know about network theory, the charge was definitely doable, and even realistic, but with considerable dangers. The Christian network did spread and was eventually embraced by the powerful, making it the most popular religion in Europe. But somewhere along the way, many in the network lost their original connection to Jesus. Instead of witnessing to what Jesus had said or done, and to his truth and grace, many became witnesses to the interpreters of who Jesus was— many degrees away from the source—resulting in the spread of many destructive things—such as hatred, exclusion, and even wars in parts of the Christian network.

Even though we are scores of generations away from the first Christians who connected directly with Jesus, faithful Christians must find ways to stay close to the source of our network—Jesus. Our first degree of connection is with the Jesus who confronted the oppressive system of his time by having relationships with the poor, the outcasts, the displaced, the unclean, and the powerless, making those who were on the fringe of the social network the center of his ministry.

The Divine-Human Network

"I am the vine, you are the branches. Those who abide in me and I in them bear much fruit, because apart from me you can do nothing... If you abide in me, and my words abide in you, ask for whatever you wish, and it will be done for you... As the Father has loved me, so I have loved you; abide in my love... This is my commandment, that you love one another as I have loved you. No one has greater love than this, to lay down one's life for one's friends. You are my friends if you do what I command you." *(John 15:5, 7, 9, 12–14)*

Jesus called his followers "friends," and invited them to abide in him and his love so that they might bear fruit. Jesus also said repeatedly that he was connected with God, who loved him, and in turn he loved them, telling them that they were to spread this love through the developing Christian network. In other words, we are only two degrees of separation from God through Jesus.

At the baptism of Jesus, the voice of God said, "You are my Son, the Beloved; with you I am well pleased" (Mark 1:11). Jesus taught us, in the Lord's Prayer, to call God "Father." The actual word that Jesus used was "*Abba,*" which was what a child would call his or her father in the language that Jesus spoke. The radical nature of Christianity as exemplified by Jesus emphasizes the parent-child relationship between human and Divine. If we are all children of God, we are all then siblings to each other. Like brothers and sisters in a family, some of us are really close; some of us might not get along well; some might really dislike each other. And yet we are family—we cannot do away with each other.

Jesus wants us to be no more than two degrees of separation from God, the Creator and Sustainer; Jesus wants us to connect with each other like brothers and sisters. With this divine-human network of grace and truth, we might be able to better understand some of the radical things that Jesus said, such as, "Love your enemy and pray for those who persecute you." Realizing and living out of this divine-human network changes every relationship. It forces us to see each other on the same level: face-to-face.

Let's do a little imagination exercise on what our community would be like if we all treated each other as siblings. Imagine that a homeless person and a millionaire are brothers; how would they relate to each other when they see each other? Imagine that a CEO of a corporation and a line worker are sisters; how would the company be run? Imagine that the marketing director of a drug manufacturer and a patient are brothers; how would a new drug be advertised? Imagine that a bank loan officer and a potential homebuyer are sisters; what would the loan process be like? Imagine that Democrats and Republicans are brothers and sisters; how would they behave in Congress?

Imagine We Are Brothers and Sisters

Invite members of your community to take a walking tour of their neighborhood. As they walk around, invite them to take notice of the people whom they see. Ask them to imagine that each person they encounter is a brother or a sister. Gather as a large group and invite participants to consider the following:

1. Select one person whom you encountered in your neighborhood. Write out a scenario or a dialogue that you would have with this person as if this person were your brother or sister.
2. Share your dialogue or scenario in small groups.
3. Consider the question: What am I called to do as a result of this reflection?

This foundational belief that we are connected to God through Jesus, making all of us closely related and interconnected like brothers and sisters, is the reason why we need to pay attention to and develop our relationships as a currency of exchange. The Christian community is called to be a network that connects people from very diverse backgrounds and experiences—man and woman, young and old, rich and poor, powerful and powerless, straight and gay, job providers and jobless, political left and political right, those who have a home and those who have none, the filled and the hungry, etc. When our churches, through our membership, make real faithful connections across the diverse people of God, we are building up the divine-human network, making everyone in the network eventually two degrees from God through Jesus. These internal and external networks of relationships are the foundational structures, the frame in which sustainable missional ministries are built.

Currency of Relationship—Internal and External

The currency of relationship consists of the internal and external networks of mutually respectful connections that leaders and members of the church or ministry have. Internal connections include constructive relationships among members and leaders, area churches or ministries of the same affiliation, area denominational organizations, and national and international denominational structures. External connections include constructive relationships with non-members, different racial, cultural and ethnic groups in the neighborhood, people with resources and people in need in the community, civic community leaders, ecumenical and interfaith partners, community and civic organizations, and local businesses.

Even though Jesus' initial network was composed mostly of Jews, he also commanded his friends to be his witnesses to the ends of the earth. Building and strengthening the internal network is an essential first step for every church. However, if we are to fulfill Jesus' command to love our neighbors as ourselves and to spread this love to the ends of the earth, we must also learn to develop relationships outside our community of faith, connecting with people in our immediate neighborhood, in the town and city, in our nation, and across the earth.

An Experience of Internal and External Networks

To demonstrate the importance of having a balance between the internal and external networks, here is an activity you can invite a group (between 8 and 30 people) to do:

1. Invite one participant to play "the outsider."
2. Invite the rest of the participants to create a body sculpture that depicts a tight-loving community.
3. Invite the outsider to attempt to join this community.
4. Invite participants to share their reflections, beginning with: "I notice...." "I wonder..."
5. Now invite participants to create a second body sculpture that depicts a community that focuses on reaching out to outsiders.
6. Invite the outsider to connect with this community. Then invite the outsider to consider finding a place inside the community to rest and to be nurtured.
7. Invite participants to share their reflections, beginning with: "I notice...," "I wonder..."
8. Invite participants to create a third sculpture that depicts a community that values both internal and external relationships.
9. Invite the outsider to join this community, find a place inside for his or her wellness, and then find a connection to exercise his or her ministry to the outside.
10. Invite participants to share what they learned from this exercise.

Developing the Currency of Relationship

Now as [Jesus and his disciples] went on their way, he entered a village where a woman named Martha welcomed him into her home. She had a sister named Mary, who sat at the Lord's feet and listened to what he was saying. But Martha was distracted by her many tasks; so she came to him and asked, "Lord, do you not care that my sister has left me to do all the work by myself? Tell her then to help me!"

But the Lord answered her, "Martha, Martha, you are worried and distracted by many things; there is need of only one thing. Mary has chosen the better part, which will not be taken away from her." *(Luke 10:38–42)*

Martha-like Ministry

Many in churches are like Martha. We are so used to "doing" church that we might neglect to be more like Mary: to be, to listen, and to relate. We've been doing this since the 1950s, when one norm of U.S. society was to go to church on Sunday morning. If a family did not go to a church of any denomination on that day, that family would be looked upon as the "other." The question of whether or not someone would come to church at all would not have even been in our consciousness. The key to church development was to compete for attendees. The thinking was like this: *If we do our music better, preach our sermons louder, and make our buildings prettier than the church down the road, people will come to our church. We just need to "do church" better, and everything will be fine.*

Most events and gatherings, as a result, are task-driven. We talk, we give instruction, and we try to convince people to stay. We plan our liturgy in a linear fashion—doing one thing at a time, making sure each piece is done well.

On Sunday morning, the ushers do their ushering by getting people to their seats. The preacher is busy getting ready to do a good sermon. The choir is practicing to do the hymns and anthem well. In many churches, the only time when there is a focus on relationship is during "the peace," which re-entered church worship in many mainline denominations during the 1970s. Even for some churches, the passing of the peace is task-driven: "Everybody stop shaking hands and hugging; we have more church to do." We forge on ahead by doing our prayers, doing communion, and doing the coffee hour. We then go home when church is done.

This is what I call a Martha-like church. Not only is our worship task-driven, we also use the Martha-like approach to many other ministries. For example, a feeding ministry that is task-driven might operate this way: We get all the donated food, we get the volunteers to come and make the food, we put the food in bags, we line up the people who come, we hand them the bag of food, then we clean up, and we are done.

In the last sixty years, the U.S. societal norm has shifted. Sunday morning is no longer set aside exclusively for church or any kind of faith-community gatherings. People no longer are necessarily expected to go to church. One of the determining factors for whether one goes to church is relationship. People go to church because they have relationships with people there, and these relationships are also exchanged for other currencies such as truth, wellness, and leadership. As our society's valuation of faith communities was shifting, many churches stayed Martha-like. Many have not learned to move from "doing" church to being a church with people who relate to people. And sixty years later, many churches are shrinking in attendance and financial resources. We need to refocus our church's ministries on being relational. In other words, we need Mary-like churches today.

Mary-like Ministry

Like Mary at the feet of Jesus in her house, a relationship-driven ministry focuses on listening. Building relationship is not a linear process but a circular or spiral one, in which we encounter another person at least a few times. Each time we get to know a little more about the person as we listen to his or her story. Each time we encounter each other, we build a little more trust.

What would a Mary-like church look like? What would our programs be like if we were focusing on building relationship as well as getting the job done? Here is an example of one church's exploration in shifting their feeding program to becoming more Mary-like during a Holy Currencies workshop. Instead of making the food for their guests, they would invite their guests to wash up and make the food together. In the process of cooking side by side, they could listen to each other's stories and build relationships. One of the members of this church was a chef of a local restaurant. They came up with another Mary-like idea: *What if we ask our chef to offer a cooking class on Wednesday when people come to the food pantry?* They noticed that some of the people had no idea how to cook the food items they got. They would invite a church member to pair up with a guest and, working together, they learned to cook a nutritious meal using exactly what was in the bag of food they received. Another church member heard of a restaurant called Soul Kitchen[6], opened by the rocker Jon Bon Jovi in central New Jersey. It is like a regular restaurant with linens and silver, and waiters, and so forth, but there are no prices on the menu. The guests make a donation for the meal. If they are unable to donate, they can volunteer to work in the kitchen. Church leaders began to envision such a ministry: *What if we create a café or restaurant like Soul Kitchen through which relationships among those who have and those who are in need could be built?*

> ## From Task to Relationship
>
> Here is an exercise in which you can engage church members to re-vision their ministries from task-driven to relationship-driven.
> 1. List some of the ministries of your church, especially the ones that involve interacting with those who are not already members of your congregation.
> 2. Spend some time discerning which approach these ministries emphasize more—are they task-driven or relationship-driven?

[6]See chapter 12 for full description of Soul Kitchen.

3. Select one of the task-driven ministries and describe what this ministry will look like (with some details) if it is a relationship-driven ministry.

For example, what would worship look like if it were relationship-driven? What would the sermon be like if it aimed at building relationships with both old-timers and the newcomers? What would the music ministry be like if its purpose was to foster connections among the worshipers? What would prayer time be like, and so on? When should we have the coffee hour? Should we just serve coffee, or should it be breakfast or lunch?

This exercise is one the most effective ways to encourage church members to begin to think missionally through simply adjusting the way they think about ministries—from doing to being with, from accomplishing tasks to building friendships, from converting someone to being a friend, from convincing to listening, from giving instructions to sharing stories, from being Martha to becoming more like Mary.

Contrasting Different Ministry Approaches

Task-Driven	Relationship-Driven
Linear	Circular or Spiral
Talking	Listening
Convincing	Trust-Building
Doing	Connecting
Instruction-Giving	Storytelling

Besides transforming your task-driven ministries into relationship-driven, here are other ways to develop your currency of relationship using other currencies that the church currently has.

Develop and Strengthen Internal-Relationships Currency

Create a special time and place on the church grounds that will enable more relationship-building among members, such as a community room, game night, regular sport events, etc. Many churches already have women's groups, men's groups, youth groups, and educational programs. To develop this currency, one might think about creating events at which interactions between these groups are encouraged. Set aside money to develop programs, events, and gatherings that strengthen internal relationships, such as relational-leadership training and pastoral-care ministries. Some churches actually hire a staff person to be the relational minister. Schedule regular times for the church members to explore and dialogue on topics on which they have different opinions and perspectives. These internal "truth events"[7] are essential for restoring relationships, especially when the church is dealing with a contentious issue. Truth events can avoid breakdown of relationships and might actually rebuild some of the already-damaged ones. Wellness events such as retreats, social events, field trips, game night, a day at the park, or visiting museums are all great events for building internal relationships. Again, the tendency might be to make these into task-oriented events; careful re-visioning and planning of these events to shift them ever-so-slightly toward relationship-driven ones will turn them into relationship-currency developmental events.

Develop External-Relationship Currency

The best way to develop external relationships is to find excuses to have a party. Wellness events for the neighborhood, such as festivals or block parties, are a great way to use your currency of time and place to develop your relationship currency. Get to know the different ethnic groups in your community. Find out what and when their significant cultural celebrations are and offer your church grounds to host these celebrations. You can get local businesses that cater to that population to be part of planning and to provide resources for these events. For example, if you have a substantive Chinese population in your neighborhood, invite the local Chinese community organizations and businesses to have a Chinese New Year celebration on your church grounds, complete with food, decorations, and the lion and dragon dances, while especially embracing the traditions that connect people, such as sharing well-wishes when you meet someone and giving red packets with money in them for the children. These celebrations do not need to be limited to that particular ethnic group. On the day of the Chinese New Year, everyone can be "Chinese" for a day. Most importantly, in order for these celebrations to be a relationship-development event, church members need to be present and ready to connect with people. Some pre-event relational-leadership training might be required. Other cultural celebrations may include a German Oktoberfest, St. Patrick's Day, English Teatime, St. Lucia Festival, the Feast of Our Lady of Guadalupe, etc. Using the church grounds, you can create relational events and social businesses such as film festivals,

---

[7]See chapter 5 on Currency of Truth for a full description of a truth event.

a laundry facility, art exhibitions, concerts, a youth theater, a flower shop, a café or restaurant, etc.

Some of these relational events and programs will require financial investments to get them started. But, if a church works through the whole Cycle of Blessings when designing these events, you might find an entrepreneurial way to make these events self-sustaining as well as relational. So set aside money in the church budget for external relationship-building events and programs; it is the best way to mobilize the Cycle of Blessings. Give money to local community and civic organizations and offer to enter into partnership with them to serve the community together—these organization may include community centers, the fire department, the library, a hospital, the human-relations commission, the YMCA, an arts center, etc. Once a month, select a local business that keeps resources flowing within the community. Invite church members to spend their money to buy something or use the services from that business. This is a smaller version of what is called "cash mob." Imagine the business owner meeting person after person coming into his or her business, all claiming to be from the same church. Over time you may develop very strong relationships with many of the local businesses.

Organizing wellness events for the community is a great way for building external relationships. Invite your neighbors to come and learn how to stay well, both spiritually and physically. Use local people, organizations, and businesses as resources; this way you are also building mutually beneficial relationships with them. Invite people in your neighborhood to come to a health fair, an emergency preparedness conference, a farmer's market, or a recycling event.

Be aware of the issues that the larger community is facing. Your church can host and facilitate "truth events" such as community forums, dialogue programs, and healing events and engage people in your community to speak the truth to each other. These kinds of gatherings are helpful in building relationships, especially when there has been a traumatic event impacting the community. Invite people in your neighborhood to come to an interracial dialogue series, interfaith dialogues, or a job fair with a strong component for dialogue between the resourceful and the unemployed.

Make sure church members commit their time to attend these events and are ready to connect and listen to people in order to make a friend. Provide leadership trainings that focus on relationship building for church members and encourage them to use these skills at these gatherings as well as at home, in school, and at work.

Relationship Currency Exchanges

During the Holy Currencies workshops, the discussion has often reverted back to money, even after I have presented the full Cycle of Blessings with all six currencies. We are so conditioned to think about sustainability with money as the only currency that some find it difficult to explore beyond the limits of what money can provide. Here is a real story of a church that unstuck itself from the tyranny of money by focusing on their currency of relationship.

This church was facing a mid-year $10,000 budget shortfall. This was not because the church was not doing missional ministries. In fact, they were serving the neighborhood with many innovative projects. During the coffee hour that Sunday, the pastor asked those gathered to bring out their phones, look through their contact lists, and select five friends who were not members of the church. The church members were invited to call the five people right then and there and tell them about the ministries of the church to the community—how they spoke the truth, built leadership, and created wellness. Then, they were to ask them for a donation. If twenty-five church members could get four out of five people to give $100, they would raise $10,000. And, indeed, within half an hour, they accomplished their task.

Instead of asking how much money they had, which then determined what ministries they could do or could not do, they asked how many relationships they had first. Since they were doing ministries that created wellness, spoke the truth, and developed leadership in the community, the people with whom they had real relationships would gladly contribute financially to support the ministry even though they were not members.

So, money is not the primary issue in most unsustainable churches. The deeper issue is relationship. If we have a strong currency of relationship—both internal and external—this currency can easily be exchanged for money and many other currencies. Let's take a closer look at the currency of relationship and how it is a principal part of the cycle of blessings.

Internal Relationships Currency Exchanges

Having strong relationships amongst members of the church is essential for a sustainable ministry. These relationships are primary to accomplishing the missional ministries of the church by being exchanged for the other five currencies.

Church members will gladly offer their volunteer hours for ministries when they have strong ties to the church community. They can also provide additional places for ministry beyond the church properties. For example, a church member might provide his or her home or business for ministries that build relationships with people in the neighborhood. Through the strong internal network of the church, raising up leaders is easily accomplished, usually by friends inviting another friend to take up leadership. Members can offer their gifts and skills for ministry, not only as individuals but also working together in teams, because of the relationships that are already developed. Strong relationships among members of the church allow people to speak truth to each other in love. They will stay together even though they might disagree and have very different perspectives on the issues they face. Their relationships will hold them together to struggle to discern the truth. Truthful relationships enable church members to stay healthy spiritually, especially when they are able to work through issues and conflicts constructively. Church members will gladly offer financial support for a church that provides them with a meaningful supportive network of relationships.

In addition to building relationships among members of the local church, denominational churches also need to maximize their relationships with area congregations of the same affiliation. Having working relationships with other churches of the same denomination will enable the churches to pool their resources of time and place, money, and gracious leadership to create and sustain ministries that can be done together while respecting the unique ministries of the separate communities. Churches in the same area can also enable each other to see the bigger picture of the needs and concerns of the larger community and to find resources to support ministry projects that the churches can do together, by speaking the truth together and creating community wellness. For the same reason, churches with denomination affiliations need to have working relationships with their national and international denominational organizations such as conferences, dioceses, conventions, presbyteries, and synods. These relationships give churches access to resources not available locally. For example, many denominational bodies can provide leadership training that will enable local churches to build relationships, speak the truth, and achieve wellness in the local communities. Sometimes a denominational body may be able to provide money and a place for a new ministry.

The key purpose to developing relationships internally is to create wellness within the church community. In that platform of spiritual, social, and sometimes financial wellness, church members can mobilize the other currencies in the Cycle of Blessings, especially in building external relationships as the prime currency for missional ministries.

Examining Your Internal Network

Gather the people in your community and invite them to examine their internal network with the following instructions:

1. Write down the names of up to five church members whom you know and trust.
2. Recall the last few contacts you had with them. What blessings were exchanged—knowledge, resources, leadership, wellness, truth, money, time, etc.?
3. Form small groups and share your insights from this examination of your internal network. (For a small congregation, another option is to ask each participant to write down his or her name on one side of a notecard, and up to five names on the other side. Using these notecards, a team of people can draw a relationship map by putting names on a large piece of paper and drawing lines representing the relationships between these names.)
4. Conclude by asking the following questions: How does your internal network shape who you are? Who are the key people in your internal network? How have you influenced your internal network through these relationships?

External Relationships Currency Exchanges

Building mutually respectful relationships with those who are not members of the church is the most important currency for missional churches. Research on the so-called emerging generation informs us that this generation wants to belong before they believe.[8] Therefore, connecting with this generation by building relationships first is the key to reaching the un-churched. Through these relationships, we discover their needs and concerns. We learn to speak the truth with them about their own experience and about their environment.

Rich and Poor

Having genuine relationships with individuals and groups in need will give us the truth of a more complete picture of what is going on in our neighborhood. On the other hand, establishing relationships with individuals, groups, and organizations that have resources are essential for balancing the sustainability equation. The church,

---

[8]See Phyllis Tickle, *The Great Emergence* (Grand Rapids: Baker Books, 2008), 158–59.

through these relationships, can connect those who have resources and those in need—challenging the resourceful ones to give and serve, while holding up the dignity of those who receive. On the other hand, spiritual wellness flows in the direction of the resourceful ones. The currencies of truth and wellness can flow from a well-developed currency of external relationship. Remember, we are talking about people who are not members of your church. The role of the church by having these relationships is to move the currencies of money, time, and place toward blessings in the wider community, creating wellness.

People from Diverse Cultural Backgrounds

Interracial conflicts and intercultural tensions are often part of the un-wellness of many communities. If members of a church have real, respectful, trusting relationships with the different racial or cultural groups in the community, we can broker many connections that would not normally occur. We can foster social wellness in the community by using our currency of relationship to bring people from different racial and cultural backgrounds to have meaningful dialogue, thereby achieving understanding, speaking truth, and building stronger community.

Civic Leaders

Do members of your church know their local, state, and federal civic leaders and elected officials—members of the school board or city council, or state senators and members of Congress, etc.? Getting to know civic leaders is vital for the church to be recognized as an essential part of the wider community. These relationships will help the civic leaders to know the concerns and issues of the neighborhood, enabling the civic leaders to do a better job in representing the people. Through these relationships, the church can be an advocate in speaking the truth to power.

Ecumenical and Interfaith Partners

Does your church have working, respectful relationships with the ecumenical and interfaith partners in your neighborhood—Protestant churches, Catholic churches, churches with no denominational affiliation, synagogues, mosques, Buddhist temples, etc.? Having mutually respectful relationships with other faith communities and organizations can be exchanged for gracious leadership so that the partners can work together to address issues that concern the wellness of the overall community. Interfaith partners may also pool financial and other resources, such as those of time and place, to address common concerns. Leadership development can also be done together, as well, by sharing cost.

Local Businesses

Do members of your church know the people working in the local grocery stores, gyms, restaurants, car services, hotels, gas stations, coffee shops, supermarkets, movie theaters, amusement parks, bookstores, major corporations, communications services, computer stores, cleaners, private healthcare providers, artists, art galleries, law firms, banks, locksmiths, accountants, etc.? These local businesses, large and small, are part of the fabric of the neighborhood. Having mutually respectful relationships with the owners and workers of these firms allows church members to listen to their concerns, let them know about the ministries of the church, and develop potential mutually beneficial community projects.

Community and Civic Organizations

Do members of your church know the people working in the local community center, post office, YMCA, library, parks, hospitals, pubic transportation agency, health centers, elderly housing complexes, children services, schools, shelters, hostels, community gardens, farmers' market, recreational facilities, public gardens, police department, fire department, courts, hospice organizations, social services, or government agencies, to name (more than) a few? When we have working relationships with these organizations, there is even more potential for working together on mutually supportive projects. It is impossible to have relationships with all of these businesses and community establishments, but the more workable relationships you have, the more possibilities your church will have in creating shared ministries for speaking the truth, creating wellness, and developing gracious leadership in the community.

Environment

Do members of your church have a deep relationship with the earth? Have they learned from nature's way of recycling and recirculating resources? Even though most of us use money to buy our food and pay for the transportation of water and energy, we need to know where our water, energy, and food come from. Having a mutually respectful relationship with the environment means knowing we are interconnected with the earth and that everything we do impacts the well being of the environment. We need to know we are part of the link of recirculating the earth's resources, and not just consumers of the same. If nature takes care of us with the abundance that it produces, how do we take care of nature? Listening to the earth and knowing what the earth needs to maintain its balance so that it can continue to regenerate itself will be exchanged for the currency of truth and wellness for all.

Examining Your External Network

Gather the people in your community and invite them to examine their external network with the following instructions:

1. Write down the names of up to five people in the wider community who are not church members and with whom you have respectful and trusting relationships.
2. Recall the last few contacts you had with them. What blessings were exchanged—knowledge, resources, leadership, wellness, truth, money, time, etc.?
3. Form small groups and share your insights from this examination of your external network. (Another option is to list all external groups and names mentioned by participants. Categorize them according to possible external relationships listed in this chapter.)
4. Conclude by asking the following questions: How does your external network shape who you are? How have you influenced your external network through these relationships? As a church community, where are your strengths in your external network? Where are we lacking in relationships in the wider community?

• • • • •

Relationship Inventory

Gather leaders of your church and take an inventory of the internal and external relationships of your church using the two tables provided in Appendix A.

Internal Relationship Inventory:

1. Name the key persons or groups who have been involved in building relationships in your internal network, whether among church members, among area churches, with area denominational organizations, or with national and international denominational structures.
2. Rate these relationships: None – weak – okay – strong
3. For what currencies and other blessings can these relationships be exchanged?

External Relationship Inventory:

1. Name the key persons or groups who have been involved in building relationships for your external network: with people not already members; with different racial, cultural, and ethnic groups in the neighborhood; with individuals and groups with resources, or individuals and groups in need; with civic and community leaders, ecumenical and interfaith partners, local businesses, civic and community organizations, and environmental groups.
2. Rate these relationships: None – weak – okay – strong
3. For what currencies and other blessings can these relationships be exchanged?

For the visual learners, draw a network map of your church or ministry based on the completed inventories of internal and external relationships. Draw a big circle on a piece of paper. Put the internal network inside the circle and the external network outside the circle. Draw lines to represent the connections among the key people and groups.

1. As you work through the two exercises, what do you notice and wonder about...
   ...where your strengths lie?
   ...where your struggles occur?
2. If you were to increase your ministry's missional effort and its sustainability:
   What do you need to pay attention to?
   What adjustment would you make to increase the effectiveness of your network, both internal and external?
3. In what ways can you assist the leaders and members of your church or ministry to increase the effectiveness of their ministry network, whether internal or external?

Develop a plan to continue to strengthen existing relationships by building up the capacity of the internal network. More importantly, develop a plan to enable church members to build mutually respectful external relationships in the areas where you are deficient.

Cornerstone and Living Stones

> The stone that the builders rejected
> has become the chief cornerstone. *(Psalm 118:22)*

A cornerstone is the first stone set in the construction of a building's foundation, from which all other stones will be set in reference, thus determining the position of the entire structure. In a human community, each person is like a stone (a living stone), connecting and supporting each other, forming a structure and a network of relationships. I have seen communities that are strong, healthy, and sustainable, characterized by a spirit of abundant living in which there is room for everyone. I have also seen communities that are not sustainable, characterized by infighting, unhealthy competitions, and a spirituality of scarcity. We can always discern why a certain community is sustainable or not by discovering the cornerstone from which the community is built.

But unlike a physical building—whose cornerstone, once laid, cannot be changed—human communities are fortunately made of living stones. We can reset the position of our community's cornerstone, thereby reorienting our community toward being missional. Jesus is the cornerstone of the church. Jesus, at the home of Martha and Mary, reminded us that relationship is the cornerstone of his community. From there, we can build the network of relationships, which is the church. When we reset the cornerstone of the church with relationships, everything is reoriented. Everything will have to be reconsidered and changed in order to strengthen internal relationships and expand our external network. We need to reorient the way we think about ministries so that everything we do has to do with building our currency of relationship in order to move toward becoming a missional and sustainable ministry.

Here are some of the ways we can help our community to reorient toward being relational by helping them notice, acknowledge, and value relationship as a currency.

Reports: The regular reports from paid staff and volunteers can include a section on relationship. For example, in a pastor's report to the church council, vestry, or session, the pastor can report what percentage of his or her time is spent on building relationships, both internal and external. The report can include the number of relationship-building events that he or she had facilitated, the number of pastoral visits, news of connections made in the community with local businesses, civic and community leaders, interfaith partners, etc.

Ministry Review: In the evaluation of every event, include a reflection on relationship building. *How did we do on building more relationships in this event?* Use the growth of relationships as a marker for the success of all programs and events. Survey newer members and ask them how they initially became connected with the church. Track the relationship networks that made that happen. Affirm and recognize individuals and groups who were keys to making these connections with newcomers.

Worship: Include a time for church members to share the new friends they made during the week and then invite the community to pray together for these new friendships. In addition to offering money, ask church members to name new relationships they have developed during the week. The community is invited to pray for these new friends by name during worship and throughout the week.

Meetings: Build into every meeting a time for relationship building.

Narrative Budget: The annual budgeting process can include a section on relationships. Categorize the different programs as internal and external relationship-building ones. The budget presentation to the congregation should also include how different budget items are important in building internal and external relationships.

Leadership Development: In every leadership-training event, include and emphasize the importance of a relational approach to ministry, making sure trainees understand that building relationships is a major part of being a leader. Include skills in listening, connecting, trust-building, and storytelling.

New Ministries: In the development and visioning of new ministries, include reflections on how the new ministry builds the internal and external relationship networks. Set relational approaches as the cornerstone of the ministry.

Expanding Your External Relationship Network

Here is an activity that you can use to develop your external network and help church members value the currency of relationship:

1. Invite church members each to consciously build respectful relationships with three people in the wider community this week—for example, get to know the gas station attendant, the head librarian, a postal worker, the school superintendent, the fire chief, the police chief, the corner grocery store owner, a janitor at the school, a homeless person at your free-lunch program, the head of a major corporation in your community, a teacher in the local college, etc.

2. Gather the group to share their experiences of attempting to start relationships in the community. Have the group share their concerns and listen to the issues they heard.
3. In addition to offering money during church worship, church members are invited to write the names of the people they have recently established relationships with on pieces of paper and put them in the offering plate as well. During prayer time, the community is invited to pray for each person by name.

CHAPTER FOUR

Boundless Compassion

"They are not just about 9 to 5 here," Neal, our tour guide said. "They really want to be your friends." He was a short ex-gang member with a tattoo of the Chinese word for "brave" on his shaved head, right behind one of his ears. I had been reading *Tattoos on the Heart* by the Rev. Gregory Boyle, S.J., a Jesuit priest, and decided to visit the Homeboy Industries headquarters in Los Angeles near Chinatown to see for myself the context of this amazing ministry that was founded on boundless compassion.

I tagged along with a tour in progress and listened to Neal's story—how he was in jail for most of his teenage years, which was where he met Father Gregory, the founder of Homeboy Industries. After he got out of jail, he got into more trouble by joining a gang, but he somehow stayed in touch with Father Greg, who consistently offered to help him. Two years ago, he finally took up his offer and went to Homeboy Industries. He got counseling; he went to anger-management classes; he even went to yoga meditation class. All of these classes were part of his job as a trainee at Homeboy Industries. He had to show up at 8:30 a.m., sign in, and be there to work and go to classes until 5 p.m., when he signed out. During that time, he had a big tattoo on his neck removed with seventeen painful treatments. He refused to tell me what the tattoo said—that was his past life, he remarked. I was glad he kept his "brave" tattoo behind his ear. He now has a steady job, he is happy, and he looks forward to going home to his daughter everyday.

Father Gregory Boyle routinely visits twenty-five detention institutions in Los Angeles County—including juvenile halls, probation camps, jails, and state youth authority facilities. He hands out his cards after celebrating Mass and says, "Call me when you get out. I'll hook you up with a job—take off your tattoos—line ya up with a counselor. I won't know where you are, but with this card, you'll know where I am. Don't slow drag. 'Cuz if you do, you'll get popped again and end up right back here. So call me."[1]

The currency of relationship that Father Greg developed with these homeboys and homegirls over the years pays off when they set foot into the place called Homeboy Industries, which now includes Homeboy Bakery, Homeboy Silkscreen, Homeboy/Homegirl Merchandise, Homeboy Diner, Homeboy Farmers Markets, and Homegirl Café. Through these social businesses[2], these young men and women receive not just jobs, but friendships—not to mention a healthy dose of leadership development skills. They begin to put their lives back together, moving steadily toward social and economic wellness. But most important of all, they discover the truth about themselves—that they are people who have gifts to offer, and that they are loved.

Tom Brokaw wrote in the foreword of *G-Dog and the Homeboys*, the first publication that told the story of Homeboy Industries, "G-Dog was their priest, confidante, tough-love counselor, advocate and, most of all, their friend, the one they could count on to treat them as people, not as statistics or inmates waiting to happen."[3]

I was so moved by my initial visit that I decided to incorporate what I experienced into the curriculum of the Kaleidoscope Summer Training Institute in Los Angeles. On a Wednesday in July, I took my class, consisting of mostly pastors and priests from the United Methodist, Presbyterian, and Episcopal churches, to Homeboy Industries for a tour. At 9 a.m., the lobby and the stairway to the second-floor offices were full of young men and women, most of whom had tattoos on their arms, necks, and shaved heads. Even though my group stood out with our middle-class clean-cut attire, everyone welcomed us with smiles and warm greetings. I realized I had no fear even though I was standing in a room full of ex-gang members, most of whom were ex-convicts. Someone announced the activities of the day, which included an anger-management class, a computer lab, an

---

[1] See Gregory Boyle, *Tattoos on the Heart* (New York: Free Press, 2010), 187.

[2] Muhammad Yunus described a "social business" as a kind of business that is "built on the selfless part of human nature" and "everything is for the benefit of others and nothing is for the owners—except the pleasure of serving humanity." I think the businesses under Homeboy Industries fit his definition very well. See Muhammad Yunus, *Building Social Business* (New York: PublicAffairs, 2010), xvii.

[3] See Celeste Fremon, *G-Dog and the Homeboys* (Albuquerque: University of New Mexico Press, 2008), x.

addiction support group, a parenting skills class, and so forth. Our group was mentioned as a tour group and they applauded. It was someone's birthday, so we sang "Happy Birthday."

Someone yelled from the stairway, "I got a job!"
Someone else asked, "In what?"
"Security," he replied with pride. Everybody applauded.

A staff member invited everyone to an upcoming picnic in the park and said, "We will play sports, but no baseball bats! Don't bring them!" Everyone laughed. Someone gave a talk that sounded a lot like a sermon about the "underdog." Someone prayed and off they went to do the work of the day.

Our tour guide, Richard, showed us the legal service, the counseling service, the job-referral department, the tattoo removal rooms, the classrooms, the bakery, and the café. When we settled into the urban garden where the café chef harvests the fresh herbs and vegetables, Richard told us his story. He told us that he just got out of federal prison sixteen months ago. He knew Father Greg some fourteen years before, when he was a teenager. He told us that he was in and out of prison for those fourteen years, and finally decided to set foot in Homeboy Industries to get his tattoos removed. That began his connection to this warm, loving, supportive, and disciplined community. Through his recovery program, Father Greg noticed that Richard was very articulate when he talked with visitors. He invited him to learn to do public speaking so he could become a motivational speaker. I was amazed at the transformation that Richard must have gone through in such a short time—all because he is now connected with a community with persistent people like Father Greg who, over a period of fourteen years, would not let him go.

On this visit, I witnessed all of the holy currencies at work in this amazing ministry. The cornerstone of Homeboy Industries is the currency of relationship. The initial contact with Father Gregory was a recurring story from almost everyone we met. The disciplined warm and welcoming community we saw during the morning meeting was infectious; I could see the newcomers relaxing after just 10 to 15 minutes sitting in this meeting. The young men and women—many for the first time—were experiencing the blessings of a supportive internal network founded on unconditional love. From this relational foundation, they are asked to commit their "time" to come to this "place" called Homeboy Industries, day after day. Richard said, "The counselor asks you to choose which classes you want," pointing to the weekly schedule, "and once you say yes, you have to come if you want to stay in the program." Throughout each day, they learn to take care of and respect both themselves and others, reconstructing their social and spiritual "wellness." They discover the "truth" as they develop their skills in working together and listening to themselves and others—even with former rival gang members. And they get paid with "money" for coming to work and taking classes re-establishing their financial "wellness." Through their work they give back by maintaining the properties and taking different roles in running the businesses, which bring in about one- third of their operating budget. They eventually develop the leadership skills that they need in order to re-enter the world as contributing members of society, thereby passing on the blessings they received.

Challenging society's perception of gang members, Father Greg said, "What if we were to invest in gang members, rather than just seek to incarcerate our way out of this problem?"[4] He mobilizes the Cycle of Blessings by taking what society throws away and reinvests them back in as valuable resources. He talks about the concept of a community of kinship, where he invites us to imagine, with God, a circle of compassion:

> Then we imagine no one standing outside of that circle, moving ourselves closer to the margins so that the margins themselves will be erased. We stand there with those whose dignity has been denied. We locate ourselves with the poor and powerless and the voiceless. At the edges, we join the easily despised and the readily left out. We stand with the demonized so that the demonizing will stop. We situate ourselves right next to the disposable so that the day will come when we stop throwing people away.[5]

---

[4]See Gregory Boyle, *Tattoos on the Heart* (New York: Free Press, 2010), 9.
[5]Ibid., 190.

CHAPTER FIVE

Currency of Truth

I am the way, and the truth, and the life. No one comes to the Father except through me. (John 14:6)

I have observed that many use the word *truth* in a polarizing way, such as *truth* versus *falsehood*, and *truth* versus *lie*. For example, John 14:6 is often interpreted in this polarizing way: Jesus is the truth, and everything and everyone else are false. Of course, this right or wrong, good or bad, either-or interpretation of the truth is often reinforced by the interpretation of the second half of the verse: "No one comes to the Father except through me." Granted, the word *truth* in the English language is often defined this way. However, the way Jesus used the word might have a different meaning stemming from his cultural background.

I often wonder why Jesus put the words "the truth" between "the way" and "the life." If Jesus wanted to use a simple either-or interpretation of "the truth," wouldn't saying, "I am the truth," be enough? Both "way" and "life" are multi-dimensional. A way is traveled through time; there is a direction, a movement from one place to another. A life is lived over a period of time in different places, and in relationships with different people. We do not take a moment in someone's life and call that "a life." A life involves a past, a present, and a future. Neither do we take one step of a journey and call that "the way." The way also has a beginning, a movement through different environments, and a destination. Perhaps the meaning of "the truth" being sandwiched in-between the multi-dimensional concepts of "the way" and "the life" ought to be understood in a similar way.

"I am the Alpha and the Omega, the first and the last, the beginning and the end." *(Revelation 22:13)*

The Hebrew word that is translated as "truth," *emet,* is composed of the three letters, א *aleph,* מ *mem,* and ת *tav*—the first, middle, and last letters of the Hebrew alphabet. The composition of the word may signify that in order to discern the truth, one must know the beginning, the middle, and the end of the event. There is no half-truth in the Hebrew *emet.* We cannot take one moment, one feeling, or one perspective and call that the truth. For this reason, we do not select one verse from the Bible and use it in a polarizing way to make judgments, calling that verse the "truth." To discern the truth we need to read the whole Bible from beginning to end.

The Chinese word for truthful or genuine, 真 *(zhén),* includes two ideograms, 十 *(shí)* and 目 *(mù).* 十 is the number ten while 目 represents the eye. The bottom part is the symbol for a table. The number ten symbolizes completeness or wholeness. Discerning the truth requires that we look at an issue or event in a wholistic way, perhaps through ten different eyes, or ten different perspectives on the table.

The Spirit of Truth

"And I will ask the Father, and he will give you another Advocate, to be with you forever. This is the Spirit of truth, whom the world cannot receive, because it neither sees him nor knows him. You know him, because he abides with you, and he will be in you." *(John 14:16–17)*

The Chinese and Hebrew essence of truth points to a comprehensive, inclusive approach to discerning the truth. This "spirit of truth" is difficult for the world to receive. We live in a world conditioned by the paradigm of either-or thinking—something is either true or false. Remember all of the "true or false" tests you took in school. Many prefer the simplistic and often adversarial approach to truth—it is easier to define the truth by proving that others lie. Remember the "You lie!" outburst of a senator during the U.S. President's State of the Union address in 2010? In that incidence, we lost the opportunity to know the truth about this senator's way of thinking and his life experience that led him to disagree with the President. Perhaps, it was easier to claim one's own experience as the only truth and thereby not have to listen to another's perspectives. The spirit of truth calls us to attempt to understand the multiple points of views. This truth-discerning process is always complex and messy.

As a Christian, I struggle with Jesus' call to love my enemy—a radical demand of the spirit of truth. I don't know the truth unless I am willing to see the conflict from my enemy's viewpoint. I am challenged to see the world from God's perspective, not just mine. God created a world where many different people and nations have their ways and lives. God loves my people and me. God also loves those whom I consider my enemies. Now what do I do?

The spirit of truth does not see the world in either-or or binary form. Technologies are not always against nature. Human action and nature's process are not always at odds with each other. Globalism and localism are not mutually exclusive. Immigrants and citizens do not have to be fearful of the other. Gay and straight are not enemies. Pro-life and pro-choice people are not necessarily adversaries. Men and women are not opposites. Archbishop Desmond Tutu said, "Differences are not intended to separate, to alienate. We are different precisely in order to realize our need of one another."[1]

In order for a community to discern the truth, it needs to take into account the different perspectives even when they seem to be opposite or contrary to each other. The truth emerges out of the exploration and understanding of the many different points of view based on different experiences of the people in the community. In the same spirit, a community also needs to know how to raise up the experiences and perspectives that might have been ignored by the dominant view. The historically dominant group has always claimed that its perspective and experience is the truth. For example, for a long time, U.S. history textbooks presented as a "fact" that Columbus discovered America. But if you ask the Native Americans, their experience of this so-called "discovery" was one of imposition, contraction of unknown diseases for which they had no defense, broken promises, and even genocide. When we simply accept the dominant point of view as the truth, we are not seeing the whole truth. We do not have the whole truth unless we also listen and understand the experiences of the historically powerless.[2] This does not mean that we ignore and put down the historically dominant point of view; it simply means that we take into account the experiences of the historically powerless first, and, in so doing, we reorient our understanding of the dominant view by putting it in a wider wholistic context. When we insist on listening and

---

[1]This is one of the more popular quotes from Archbishop Desmond Tutu. I found it on the website www.goodreads.com at *http://www.goodreads.com/quotes/show/132838.*

[2]For a full exploration on the concept of what I called "divine truth," see Eric H. F. Law, *The Word at the Crossings* (St. Louis: Chalice Press, 2004), 53–74.

presenting additional points of view, this may put us into conflict with those who still live in the either-or, right or wrong, true or false, good or bad, saint or sinner world. But this might be the cost of following the spirit of truth, seeing the world as God sees it—with ten eyes, from alpha to omega.

Jesus is the way, the truth, and the life. In order for us to truly understand what it means to believe that Jesus is the truth, we have to know the beginning, the middle, and the end of Jesus' life. By the way, the end in Jesus' story is also the beginning of his resurrection. In order for us to know the truth, we have to follow Jesus' way—his action, his pattern of behavior in connecting with the poor and powerless of his time, his challenges to the powerful and rich, his way of laying his life down for others, his way of entering into the destruction of human fear and emerging triumphantly with love and grace. In order to discern the truth, we need to live a life patterned after Jesus'—his relationships with his humble and courageous earthly parents, his acceptance of his calling, his recognition of his divinity, his compassion for the powerless and poor, his sharing of his power and authority with his friends, his boldness to challenge the system with love, his sharing of God's abundance, his courage to face suffering and death, and his unshakable belief in the resurrection. Jesus' life is the way to follow and the life to live, in order for us to be the truth. Truth is a way of being—a journey, a process, a spirituality, a relationship with God through Christ, a way to see the world as God sees it, and a way that leads to action to restore the blessings that flow from God to all.

Discerning the Truth Around an Internal Issue

1. Select an internal issue with which your church or ministry is currently struggling.
2. List the people whose perspectives are important to include in order for your church or ministry, and your leaders and members, to discern the truth.
3. Circle the ones on the list whom you consider powerless and voiceless in your church or ministry. The powerless ones are usually the ones at the fringe of your network. Put yourself in the powerless persons' positions and describe the issue as they might have experienced it. (If possible, listen to these persons first and write down their experiences of the issue.)

4. Write down your understanding of the issue from the perspectives of the powerful. 5. How does attempting to understand the issue from the perspectives of the powerless first affect your understanding of the issue?

5. Write an imaginary dialogue with two or more voices representing the various perspectives. Allow the dialogue to go on until there might be a resolution.

• • • • •

Discerning the Truth Around an External Issue

1. Select an external community issue with which your church or ministry is currently struggling.

2. List the people whose perspectives are important to include in order for your church or ministry, and your leaders and members, to discern the truth. The list can include individuals and groups from within the church and outside in the wider community.

3. Circle the ones on the list whom you consider powerless and voiceless in the community. The powerless ones are often the ones located at the fringe of the community network. Put yourself in the powerless persons' positions and describe the issue as they might have experienced it. (If possible, listen to these persons first and write down their experiences of the issue.)

4. Write down your understanding of the issue from the perspectives of the powerful.

5. How does attempting to understand the issue from the perspectives of the powerless first affect your understanding of the issue?

6. Write an imaginary dialogue with two or more voices representing the various perspectives. Allow the dialogue to go on until there might be a resolution.

Developing Currency of Truth

The currency of truth is the ability to articulate individually and corporately the global and wholistic truth, internally (the experiences of the different individuals and groups within the church or ministry) and externally (the experiences of the different individuals and groups in the community, the neighborhood, the city or town, the nation, and the earth).

> When the Spirit of truth comes, he will guide you into all the truth; for he will not speak on his own, but will speak whatever he hears, and he will declare to you the things that are to come. *(John 16:13)*

Developing our currency of truth requires that we have the ability to recognize processes that are incomplete, partial, and divisive, and replace them with wholistic truth-seeking processes—from debate mode to dialogue mode, from premature judgment to clarification before judgment, from convincing to mutual understanding, from my-truth-versus-your-truth to shared truth, from mono-perspective to multi-perspectives, from either-or to both-and, from sinner or saint thinking to we-are-all-sinners-and-saints, from who is right to what is right, from accepting the viewpoint of the powerful to raising up the voices of the powerless, from standing in the center to circling around the margin, from divisive solutions to community-owned resolution, from denigrating differences to being curious about differences, and from targeting the other as the evil one to naming the unjust system. When we are able to make this adjustment in designing every event, meeting, and gathering, the people with whom we have contact will learn and experience consistently the truth-seeking way. And our community will live a life that is guided by the spirit of truth in everything that we do.

Add Truth to Everything You do

Here is an exercise with which church leaders can engage their members to re-vision their ministry to incorporate truth-discernment as part of their goals.

1. List the ministries that your church community currently has.
2. Take each ministry and redesign it so that at each meeting, event, and gathering, there will be a time for discernment of the truth. This would most likely mean incorporating a process that will allow the sharing of different perspectives and experiences, beginning with the perceived powerless. See the chart below, distinguishing the difference between an "incomplete and partial process" and a "wholistic truth-seeking process."

For example, what would a truth-seeking worship service look like? What powerless voices should be part of the expression of worship, and how? What would the music ministry be like if it seeks to tell the truth of the different populations in your church and in the wider community? What would a truth-revealing sermon sound like? What would prayers for the truth be like, and who should be the ones to voice them? For internal ministries, what would the men's group gathering be like? What would the women or children or youth ministry events be like? Who should speak first and who should listen first? How would truth-seeking decisions be made in the meetings of these groups? For external ministries, what would your truth-seeking outreach programs be like? To whom in your neighborhood would you listen to in order to discern the greater truth of justice issues? What would discerning the truth during a food program be like?

3. Make a list of doable redesigned meetings, events, and gatherings that you will implement in the coming year.

4. Create a leadership-development program to train church members to engage in discerning the truth during these upcoming redesigned truth-seeking events.

Incomplete and Partial Process	Holistic Truth-Seeking Process
Debate	Dialogue
Convincing	Mutual understanding
My truth vs. your truth	Our truth
Either-or	Both-and
Premature judgment	Clarification before judgment
Acquiescence to the powerful	Listen to the powerless first
Mono-perspective	Multi-perspective
Put down differences	Be curious about differences
Divisive solution	Community-owned resolution

Truth Events

A church in an urban setting has worked hard for ten years to become a multicultural church. On any given Sunday, there is an

English-language, a Korean-language, and a Spanish-language worship service. For a long time, a major part of the financial security of the church came from the rental of a building they owned. In 2011, the tenant decided to move and there was no prospect for a new renter. The cost to fix the building in order to make the building more rentable was too high. Without the income from the rent, the financial projection for the rest of the year was grim. The church council, which consisted of a majority of English-speaking European Americans, decided that the fiscally responsible thing to do was to sell the building. Once the announcement was made, leaders and members of both the Korean- and Spanish-language ministries expressed major concerns.

The Kaleidoscope Institute was called in to assist. The request was for us to help them decide whether they should sell or not sell. However, as we discussed how we would address their concerns, we agreed that this was not simply an either-or matter but a more complex multi-perspective issue. We proposed a series of truth events consisting of four evening dialogues involving all language groups. Here are the outlines of each session:

- Session One invited church members to explore and gain a deeper understanding of their history together. The process included asking each language group to create a timeline of their part of the ministry. They were invited to describe the strengths and struggles of each period in their histories and then report back to the whole group. We invited the Spanish-speaking group to share first, then the Korean-speaking group, and finally the English-speaking group. Participants left this session with a very positive sense of their accomplishments as a truly multicultural community, recognizing the sacrifices that many had made and the generosity they shared.
- Session Two invited participants to examine the church's present state of operation. Again, in separate language groups, they were invited to describe how the church functioned—how communication was done and decisions were made. Again, the Spanish-speaking group was invited to share first, followed by the Korean-speaking group, and finally the English-speaking group. By this time, the English-speaking group was getting restless. They asked, "When are we going to get to the meat?" This meant when were we going to make the decision of whether to sell or not to sell?
- Session Three invited them once again to go into three language groups and discuss what the impact of the decision to sell the building had on their part of the ministries. When they

returned, again, the Spanish-speaking group went first. They expressed their disappointment in how they were not informed about the financial trouble until they heard about the sale of the building. They believed they were full members of the church and should have shared the burden. They closed their sharing with, "Never underestimate what tamales can do." And the whole gathering laughed. I noticed an uneasy reaction from the Spanish-speaking group and asked them how they felt about the laughing reaction to their "tamales" remark. They said what they meant was that they could really help financially by making and selling food, and this was a very serious matter. (Subsequently, they indeed, started a tamale ministry and were bringing in about $500 per week.) Then the Korean-speaking group shared that they were brought up tithing 10 percent of their income. They had been growing in number steadily and they would need the additional rooms for their expanding ministries. So selling the building did not make sense to them. If they continued to grow at the same rate, they estimated that the financial income in the next year would be quite enough to make up for the financial shortfall. Also, they expressed their concerns about not being consulted on the sale of the building, as they were also full members of the church. Finally, when the English-speaking group reported, there was not much more that needed to be said.

- Session Four invited them to discern what they should do. They decided not to sell the building and work together as one community to get through this difficult financial period.

One year later, the church was financially stable, with the Korean-language ministry continuing to grow as expected. The new issue that church needed to address was whether they had the money to hire a full-time pastor for the Spanish-language ministry, since the last pastor, who was part-time, had retired. This time, there was a real cooperation in working through this issue. They decided that the fair and just thing to do was to offer a full-time position and they promised to work hard to find the money together to make it happen. Their investment in developing their currency of truth a year ago was now paying off by now being exchanged for financial and social wellness.

Developing our currency of truth often involves noticing a concern or issue that is emerging for the church or for the wider community. When we notice such an issue, especially the ones that are potentially divisive, the church needs to mobilize its resources to create a truth event. A truth event, like the example of the church described above, can be a series of gatherings, a one-time event, a one-on-one or in small groups, or it can be an internal personal-reflection process in thinking through an issue. Remember that discerning the truth is a process. It takes time—it may involve a place where we do the discernment, it takes gracious leadership, it takes strong relationship, it takes spiritual and social wellness, and sometimes it takes money to coordinate and support such truth events.

Here are some more ideas for developing your church's currency of truth. Gracious leadership is the most important currency that you can use to develop your currency of truth. Knowing how to use inclusive tools such as Respectful Communication Guidelines, Mutual Invitation, Kaleidoscope Bible Study, and the Grace Margin are essential for creating truth events.[3] For example, the next time your church is facing a potentially divisive issue, leaders need to know how to use these skills and processes to enable members with different perspectives to dialogue and achieve understanding before making a decision.

Having trusting relationships goes a long way to develop your currency of truth. When you have pre-established respectful relationships with people in the community—local civic and community leaders; local businesses; the diverse populations in your neighborhood such as rich and poor, young and old, and different ethnic groups—you can invite individuals and groups to truth events, and people will come.

Wellness events such as church retreats, community health fairs, local economic summits for the community, and field trips to discern the wellness of the environment are platforms for developing your currency of truth as well. When the church has been part of fostering physical, social, economic, and ecological wellness in the community (which means your currency of wellness is strong), people will be more likely to accept an invitation to come to a truth event.

Invite church members to commit time, money, and place to create truth events for church members and the community. Immersion experiences, such as taking time to experience living in another cultural environment, are great ways to help participants to gain a fuller perspective of the truth. For example, the youth and young adults of a church were trying to raise money for a not-for-profit agency that aided needy children. In order to do that, the young people chose to experience "30 Hours of Famine." They began fasting at noon Friday and planned to continue 30 hours, until 6 p.m. Saturday. They drank

---

[3]See chapter 9, on Gracious Leadership, for detailed description of these tools.

only water through the fast and slept outdoors in sleeping bags or on boxes (with adult supervision, of course). They said they wanted to experience what it was like to be hungry and homeless for a day. The young people raised money from friends and family in conjunction with the fast and sleep-out. The weekend also involved community service and shopping for nonperishable items for the "Street Outreach" program of the agency. By purposefully putting themselves in the experiences of the other, the young people got a glimpse of the truth of the experience of the hungry and homeless. Using this currency of truth, they were able to raise both the money and the consciousness of the wider community. More importantly, the currency of truth—their experience—will stay with them for the rest of their lives.

Offer your place and gracious leadership to host truth events such as community forums; pre- and post-election discussions; interracial, intercultural, and intergenerational dialogues; or interfaith dialogues. If your church is consistently the place where the truth can be discerned, people in the community will come, knowing that their experiences and perspectives will be valued. They will want to maintain their relationships with people in your ministry because sharing the truth will lead to reconciliation, constructive resolution, and wellness. They will be open to contributing their money, their time, and their talent to support your ministry.

Create a Truth Event

Select either an internal or an external issue. Create an event or program that brings together the powerful and the powerless for dialogue.

1. Give the event a neutral name and a time frame that is acceptable to most people whom you want to invite.
2. Discern which individuals or groups are perceived as powerful regarding this issue. Discuss how you would invite and prepare them to come to this event; be ready to listen first, and then share their perspectives.
3. Discern which individuals or groups are perceived as powerless regarding this issue. Discuss how you can build trusting relationships with them and prepare them to come to this event; be ready to share their perspectives.
4. Decide what resources you will need in order to facilitate this event: facility, leadership, finances, etc.
5. At the event, what will you do to make sure that the powerless get to share first and the powerful are invited to listen?

Truth Currency Exchanges

The currency of truth flows naturally into wellness and relationship. Internally, the ability to discern the truth—enabling members to listen and understand the diverse perspectives within the community—will enable members to strengthen their relationships with each other. Sometimes it will also restore their spiritual and social wellness through reconciliation, healing, and forgiveness. When your church is a place where truth is spoken, members learn and increase their leadership capability to continue to propagate the truth at home, in school, at work, and in their social circles.

When church members utilize their ability to assist the wider community to discern the truth by facilitating the listening to and hearing of diverse experiences and perspectives that exist in the community, we strengthen our relationships with the diverse populations and build bridges across the different groups and individuals in the community. When diverse populations and individuals encounter each other's truth, there might be reconciliation, healing, and even forgiveness, fostering spiritual and social wellness in the community. Furthermore, in an event where the resourceful and those in need are speaking the truth to each other, we might restore the flow of money, creating financial wellness in the community. Truth, as a currency, will further develop not only church members' ability to speak the truth, it will also enable others in your neighborhood, town, or city to embrace this wholistic way of discerning the truth, especially when the community is dealing with divisive issues.

The currency of truth challenges church members to rethink how they use their money, time, and the places to which they have access. It also ignites church members' passion for justice. As a result of experiencing this truth-seeking way, church members may decide to dedicate more of their volunteer time for truth work. They may offer the places to which they have access for hosting truth events for the church and for the community to address community issues such as interracial tension, at-risk youth, joblessness, homelessness, economic crisis, political divisions, etc. Ultimately, the ability to discern the truth with the neighborhood, town, city, or even wider environment will create social, economic, and ecological wellness.

Truth Inventory

Gather leaders of your church and take an inventory of your currency of truth using the chart provided in Appendix A.

1. Internally, what has your church done in the last year to enable church members to discern the truth? In what ways has your church engaged members to dialogue and understand the different perspectives on internal issues, especially in the decision-making process?

2. Externally, what has your church done in the last year to assist the wider community— neighborhood, city, or town—to discern the truth, especially when the community was facing issues of impact? In what ways has your church provided opportunities (truth events) for members of the wider community to dialogue and achieve understanding of the different perspectives of community issues, moving toward the possibility of a constructive and faithful resolution? These issues might be on immigration, sexual orientation, political debates, economic injustice, interfaith concerns, interracial tension, environmental concerns, etc. What has your church done to enable the people of your community to listen to the earth and discern the truth about the environment?

3. Make a list of the "truth events" that your church has facilitated in the last year.

4. Further explore which currencies these truth events exchanged—wellness, relationship, leadership, money, time and place, or truth? Remember that it is the exchange of these currencies that gives them value.

5. As you complete the inventory, what do you notice and wonder about...
   ...where your strengths are?
   ...where your struggles are?

6. If you were to increase your church's sustainability and missional effort, what do you need to pay attention to? What adjustment would you make to increase your church's ability to discern the truth internally and externally?

7. In what ways can you assist the leaders and the members of your church to increase their ability to be truth-seeking people?

8. Develop a plan to further develop your church's currency of truth addressing internal and external issues in the coming year.

Valuing Truth as a Currency

For most church members, thinking of truth as a currency is probably not something that they are accustomed to. Yet, currency of truth is the heart of missional ministry. Truth allows church members to be authentically themselves, and at the same time enables them to appreciate others as authentically themselves. It is through the truthful and authentic encounter of each other that relationships are built.

Currency of truth is what ignites the passion behind the justice work in which church must engage in order for the church to be relevant in restoring the spiritual, economical, and social wellness in our communities. In order to move our church members toward thinking and being missional, we need to implement ways to help our community to notice, acknowledge, and value truth as a currency. We need to show how we measure the development and the exchange of this currency.

Truth about the Unemployed

Gather both the unemployed and the employed together for a truth event.

1. Invite those who are looking for work to sit in a circle in the middle of the room. Invite the rest to sit in an outer circle.
2. Invite the inner circle to share their experiences of being unemployed and having to look for work. Invite the outer circle to listen without comments until everyone in the inner circle has had a chance to share.
3. Invite the participants in the outer circle to respond by completing the sentences: I noticed... I wonder...
4. Invite participants, as a large group, to consider: As a community with employed and unemployed people, what can we do together to share the truth?

Reports: Regular reports from paid staff and volunteers should include a section on truth. For example, in a pastor's report to the church council, vestry, or session, the pastor can report what percentage of his or her time is spent on developing the currency of truth, both internal and external. The report can include the number of truth events that he or she had facilitated, plus the number of truth encounters within the church membership and with people in the wider community such as local businesses, civic and community leaders, interfaith partners, etc.

Narrative Budget: The annual budgeting process can include a section on truth. Categorize the different programs as internal and external truth events. The budget presentation to the congregation should also include an explanation of budget items for truth events and why they are important to the mission of the church.

Meetings: Build into every meeting and gathering a truth-telling time.

Leadership Development: In every leadership-training event, incorporate skills for creating and facilitating a truth event such as Grace Margin, Respectful Communication Guidelines, Kaleidoscope Bible Study, etc. Provide periodic truth events for the church members, especially when there have been conflicts and tension within the church. Provide periodic truth events for church members to interact with people in the wider community. Teach church members to be present and listen to others' stories as a way to discern the truth.

Ministry Reviews: Evaluate every event using the currency of truth as an indicator for success. Include a reflection on how this event presents the truth for those who attended. Did people leave this event not only knowing just their own perspectives, but also the perspectives and experiences of others?

Worship: Conscious inclusion of the powerless voices in the leadership, prayers, sermon, music, art, and images during worship are essential ways of inviting your church members to value the process of living the truth. More importantly, point out that the way we do our worship is the way and the life of discerning the truth.

New Ministries: In the development and visioning of new ministry, include reflection on how this ministry speaks the truth in the church and in the wider community. Incorporate the truth-seeking way into the life of the new ministry from the start.

Truth-Seeking Community

1. Select an issue that the church or the community is facing. Invite church members to consciously listen to at least three people with different perspectives in the community. The objective is not to agree with these perspectives, but to simply listen and understand and record them. The invitation can be issued during worship.

2. Gather the community to share what they have heard. Invite the community to listen and ask clarifying questions to achieve full understanding of the different perspectives. This can be incorporated as part of the sermon or prayer time during worship a week later.

> 3. Invite participants to reflect on and complete the following sentence and share: *As a result of understanding the different perspectives on this issue, God is calling me to...* Participants can write their sentences on notecards and put them in the offering plate during the offertory in worship.

The Truth Will Set You Free

Seven hundred protesters were arrested during a march blocking traffic on the Brooklyn Bridge for several hours on October 1, 2011. They were part of the movement called *Occupy Wall Street* that had been camping out in a plaza in Manhattan's Financial District for nearly two weeks, speaking out against corporate greed.

Their voice was represented by slogans such as, "Wall Street got bailed out, and we all got sold out!" and, "Ninety-nine percent of the people need to be prospering, not just the top one percent." These chants finally got airtime on news programs across the United States. It started out with just a handful of protesters near Wall Street, initially described as being "ragtag" and "disorganized." However, as the protests grew larger and sprouted new protests in other cities across the nation, more and more people took notice of this truly grass-roots movement—a movement without any backing from behind-the-scenes big-money people with a political agenda.

All the discussions and actions around fixing our economy had centered around money as if it were the only currency that matters—the bailout of banks and automobile companies, to tax or not to tax, to cut or not to cut government programs, how to take money from this and give it to that in order create more jobs, etc. Yet the U.S. economy still had not recovered. Perhaps focusing on the currency of money was not the best strategy to get our resources flowing again in our nation and communities.

The Occupy Wall Street movement utilized another currency in their action—a currency that was more powerful than money—a currency called truth. By voicing the "truth" as experienced by the powerless, they provided a counter-version of the truth of our economy as projected by the rich and powerful. We do not have the whole truth of any issue until we have heard from the powerless amongst us. By taking action in speaking the truth, investing their time by occupying a strategic place, the Occupy Wall Street movement was forcing a relationship with the media, the political players, and hopefully the financial sectors, not only in New York but also across the nation. The currency of truth also fostered connections among all the protest groups as they sprung up across the country, thanks to powerful social media providing a ready-made global network that continued to feed and support local actions, even after most of the occupation of physical places had been disbanded.

The success of this movement depends on how they continue to use the currency of truth, which has already been exchanged for the currency of relationships. To achieve national financial and social wellness, this movement will need to develop its currencies of gracious leadership—leadership that could utilize the newly forged relationships to gather, nurture, and amplify the voices of the powerless, help them define common goals, and find time and places for focused strategic actions. They also need leadership that can pull the powerful—politicians and corporate players—into the conversation, helping them to truly listen.

The most profound realization that any powerful person or group in any society can have is that, without the cooperation of the powerless, their power disappears. This is why blocking the Brooklyn Bridge, resulting in 700 arrests, was so effective in getting the attention of the powerful. What would happen if all the unemployed people (at least 14 million people at that time) got on the street and blocked all of the roads and doorways to banks and financial corporations? The whole financial system would shut down! This is the ultimate truth. When the rich and powerful realize this truth, they will listen and may loosen up their hold on money and other resources and let them flow again. The truth is that in order for our community to be sustainable, resources must flow equitably and freely so that *all* may prosper, not just the one percent.

> We must no longer be children, tossed to and fro and blown about by every wind of doctrine, by people's trickery, by their craftiness in deceitful scheming. But speaking the truth in love, we must grow up in every way into him who is the head, into Christ, from whom the whole body, joined and knit together by every ligament with which it is equipped, as each part is working properly, promotes the body's growth in building itself up in love. *(Ephesians 4:14–16)*

CHAPTER SIX

Feeding the Multitudes

After the 1974 famine in Bangladesh, Muhammad Yunus, an academician in the field of economics, found it increasingly difficult to teach economic theories in the classroom. He decided to go to Jobra, a neighboring village outside of Chittagong University, to be with the distressed people there. This was his first step to seeking the truth.

In the village of Jobra, he was shocked to discover that forty-two very poor families had borrowed a total of 856 taka (roughly $27 U.S.) from the moneylenders. These moneylenders virtually enslaved them with high interest and unfair conditions imposed on the loans. He wrote in his book, *Building Social Business*, "To free these forty-two people from the clutches of the moneylenders, I reached into my own pocket and gave them the money to repay the loans. The excitement that was created in the village by this small action touched me deeply. I thought, 'If this little action makes so many people so happy, why shouldn't I do more of this?'"[1]

So he tried for several months to convince local banks to lend money to the poor, but they all refused on the grounds that the poor were not credit worthy. He then offered to become a guarantor for the loans to the poor and was successful in getting the loans from the bank. Acting as an informal banker, he came up with a few simple rules, "such as having people repay their loans in small weekly amounts and having the bank officer visit the villagers rather than making the villagers visit the bank. These ideas worked. People paid back the loans on time, every time."[2]

---

[1]See Muhammad Yunus, *Building Social Business* (New York: PublicAffairs, 2010), viii.
[2]Ibid., ix.

After encountering more difficulties in expanding the program through existing banks, he decided to create a separate bank for the poor. This was the beginning of Grameen Bank, or "village bank," in the Bengali language. By 2010, Grameen Bank lent out over $100 million a month in collateral-free loans, serving the poor in every single village of Bangladesh. The bank is actually owned by the borrowers, who, as shareholders, elect nine of the thirteen members of the board of directors. Grameen Bank even lends to beggars. In four years since the launching of this program, over 18,000 have quit begging. Grameen Bank offers affordable loans for children of borrowers to go to school. More than 50,000 students have benefited from these loans, pursuing education in medical schools, engineering schools, and universities. These young people were encouraged to develop their entrepreneurial leadership by pledging "they will never enter the job market to seek jobs from anybody. They'll be job givers, not job seekers."[3] Grameen Bank is financially self-sustaining, with all of its funds coming from deposits. The borrowers are required to save a little bit every week, and their collective savings amount to over half a billion U.S. dollars. Grameen Bank and Muhammad Yunus were the winners of the Nobel Peace Prize in 2006.

There are Grameen-type programs in almost every country in the world, including the United States. Grameen America opened its first branch in Queens, New York, in 2008. Its mission is to provide "affordable micro-loans to financially empower low-income entrepreneurs." Its vision is "to help create a world free of poverty. We predict a market where *any* individual with a dream can receive affordable financial products regardless of income, previous credit history, education, or business experience. We envision a world where burgeoning entrepreneurs are empowered to lift themselves out of poverty through hard work and determination to forge better lives for their families and future generations."[4]

I wanted to find out how all this worked. So I e-mailed the Queens branch of Grameen America, asking to speak with someone. To my surprise, a project manager called me back. She was friendly and open to answering any questions I had. I wanted to know how the loan process worked and how they work with loan recipients in sustaining their new businesses and repaying their loans. I discovered that the key to the extremely high repayment rate was in keeping a relationship with the

---

[3]Ibid., x–xi.
[4]From the Grameen America website: http://www.grameenamerica.com/about-us/mission-and-values/mission-and-vision.html

borrower and in leadership development. As far as I could tell, there was no fixed process for the loan application. The bank loan officers get to know the applicants personally, find out about their business ideas, and even help them create a sustainable business plan. Once the borrower's loans are approved, they are required to attend weekly meetings with other loan recipients. During these meetings, which are facilitated by a bank employee, they support each other's efforts, learn more business skills, and repay a small amount of their loan. The development of the currency of relationship and leadership in Grameen's loan process was a revelation to me. In other words, giving money alone—without relationships and nurturing leadership—does not create wellness.

> When it grew late, his disciples came to him and said, "This is a deserted place, and the hour is now very late; send them away so that they may go into the surrounding country and villages and buy something for themselves to eat." But he answered them, "You give them something to eat." They said to him, "Are we to go and buy two hundred denarii worth of bread, and give it to them to eat?" And he said to them, "How many loaves have you? Go and see." When they had found out, they said, "Five, and two fish."… Taking the five loaves and the two fish, he looked up to heaven, and blessed and broke the loaves, and gave them to his disciples to set before the people; and he divided the two fish among them all. And all ate and were filled, and they took up twelve baskets full of broken pieces and of the fish. Those who had eaten the loaves numbered five thousand men. *(Mark 6:35–38, 41–44)*

We call this a miracle because we cannot understand how five loaves and two fish can feed more than 5000 people and still leave twelve baskets of leftovers. But after knowing the story of the Grameen Bank, such a miracle can happen—and is still happening. Muhammad Yunus responded to the call to do something about the poverty ("You give them something to eat") by offering $27 worth of loans for the poor people of Jobra. In twenty-five years, this meager amount has multiplied into wellness for countless individuals, families, and communities, with plenty of extra leftovers.

How will you respond to Jesus' challenge, "You give them something to eat," today?

Yunus, now a famous Nobel Prize winner, was invited to meet with the CEO of Adidas, who wanted to understand the concept of social businesses, which Yunus described as a kind of business that is "built on the selfless part of human nature" and in which "everything is for the benefit of others and nothing is for the owners—except the pleasure of serving humanity."[5] The question arose as to what Adidas could do to address a pressing social problem. He said, "Maybe Adidas can start with a statement of commitment, something like this: Nobody in the world should go without shoes. As a shoe company, it is our responsibility to make shoes affordable even to the poorest person."[6] The CEO of Adidas agreed that this statement made sense and wanted to meet with his senior colleagues to discuss this idea. Later that day, they met again and he asked Yunus how cheap the shoes would have to be in order for them to be affordable to the poorest. The response, "Maybe under one dollar or so, I guess." Yunus thought this was the end of their conversation, but, to his surprise, the CEO of Adidas, at the end of the meeting, declared that the Adidas Group would join Yunus's organization to launch a social business to produce shoes for the poor in Bangladesh for a price as close as possible to one euro.

Activated by the truth, Yunus lived the Cycle of Blessings. His passion and success in serving the poor and eliminating poverty began with his yearning to understand the experiences of the poor. This currency of truth that he gained from seeing the world from the eyes of the poor moved him to invest a modest amount of money to create wellness for others. Using his academic studies in economic theories, he created an institution through which the poor and disenfranchised can connect with financial resources and build relational networks that support them and keep them accountable to each other, further nurturing their economic, social, and physical wellness. Using creative ways of circulating money, his organization raised up leaders through education and scholarships. These leaders continue to spread truth and wellness throughout their communities, contributing to the Cycle of Blessings.

As his reputation spread, he built relationships with other leaders of business corporations such as BASF, Danone, and Uniqlo. Using this currency of relationship, he spoke the truth to the powerful and those who were resource-rich, and challenged them to act outside the box of profit-making and resource-depleting businesses and venture into the world of abundance-sharing by using the same business skills and knowledge, and, in the process, foster wellness for a multitude of people in the world.

---

[5]See Muhammad Yunus, *Building Social Business* (New York: PublicAffairs, 2010), xvii.
[6]Ibid., 186.

And what does the L<small>ORD</small> require of you,
but to do justice, and to love kindness,
and to walk humbly with your God? *(Micah 6:8)*

From Truth to Action

1. Invite members of your church to take a walking tour of the neighborhood.
2. Ask participants to notice individuals and groups that are on the margins of the community—the powerless and voiceless.
3. Gather participants. List the individuals and groups whom they observed to be on the margins of the neighborhood.
4. Form small groups and invite each group to take one of the marginal persons or groups and discuss how they can find out the truth about that person's or group's story—their concerns, struggles, values, and gifts.
5. Invite each group to report their ideas. Create a plan based on these ideas to develop your currency of truth.

CHAPTER SEVEN

Currency of Wellness

How do you know your body is not well? What are the external signs? What are the internal causes for the body not being well? These are the questions we ask in diagnosing the health of our bodies. The human body's wellness depends on a number of interconnected systems: the muscular, skeletal, nervous, respiratory, and digestive systems, among others. The most important of all the systems is the circulatory system, which is an organ system that passes nutrients, gases, hormones, blood cells, etc., to and from cells in the body to help fight diseases and to help stabilize body temperature and pH to maintain homeostasis. The other major part of wellness has to do with the cycle of work and rest—when we are awake, we are doing things, exercising and moving the different systems; when we are asleep, all the systems rest and restore themselves. Using the body as an analogy for community, we can also ask: What are the different cycles and systems that make up a healthy, missional, and sustainable community? We also need to know whether the community has a balance between rest and work.

Sabbath—The Key to Wellness

Observe the sabbath day and keep it holy, as the LORD your God commanded you. Six days you shall labor and do all your work. But the seventh day is a sabbath to the LORD your God; you shall not do any work—you, or your son or your daughter, or your male or female slave, or your ox or your donkey, or any of your livestock, or the resident alien in your towns, so that your male and female slave may rest as well as you. Remember that you were a slave in the land of Egypt, and the LORD your God brought you out from there with a mighty hand and an outstretched arm; therefore the LORD your God commanded you to keep the sabbath day. *(Deuteronomy 5:12–15)*

For six years you shall sow your land and gather in its yield; but the seventh year you shall let it rest and lie fallow, so that the poor of your people may eat; and what they leave the wild animals may eat. You shall do the same with your vineyard, and with your olive orchard. *(Exodus 23:10–11)*

Every seventh year you shall grant a remission of debts. And this is the manner of the remission: every creditor shall remit the claim that is heldagainst a neighbor, not exacting it of a neighbor who is a member of the community, because the LORD's remission has been proclaimed. *(Deuteronomy 15:1–2)*

You shall count off seven weeks of years, seven times seven years, so that the period of seven weeks of years gives forty-nine years. Then...you shall have the trumpet sounded through all your land. And you shall hallow the fiftieth year and you shall proclaim liberty throughout the land to all its inhabitants. It shall be a jubilee for you: you shall return, every one of you, to your property and every one of you to your family. That fiftieth year shall be a jubilee for you: you shall not sow, or reap the aftergrowth, or harvest the unpruned vines. For it is a jubilee; it shall be holy to you: you shall eat only what the field itself produces. *(Leviticus 25:8–12)*

The weekly Sabbath, the sabbatical year, and the Jubilee year, as described in the Bible passages above, are key to creating a sustainable healthy community and, in the Judeo-Christian context, they are commanded by God for the human community to follow. They provide an overall rhythm for work and rest—every seven days, everybody rests, including the animals. Every seven years, we cancel debts and let the earth rest as well. The most radical of all is the prescription of the Jubilee year—every fiftieth year, not only do we let the earth rest, and forgive everyone's debt, we also let people have a home and family to return to. That is, every fiftieth year we start over—socially, economically, and ecologically.

God knows that in every human community, no matter how egalitarian its beginnings might be, the circulation of financial and other resources and power in social relationships will eventually become uneven. Some will suffer; others will continue to prosper. The institutions of the Sabbath, the sabbatical year, and Jubilee are God's way of ensuring that economical, financial, and ecological resources will recover their healthy circulation. Just as the circulatory system of the human body brings nutrients and energy to every part of the body, God longs for the human community to have a healthy circulation of our resources, reaching not just the powerful and rich of our society but everyone.

Furthermore, God also anticipates that humankind, in our working and consuming the fruits of the land, might obstruct the rejuvenation cycles of the earth. Thus, God insists that we let the land rest as part of the restoring of the flow between the earth and human society. Even though the concept of Jubilee has never been fully realized, it remains the most powerful command for human communities to move toward wellness physically, socially, economically, and ecologically. By doing so, we can be spiritually healthy. This was why the first thing that Jesus did at the beginning of his ministry was to proclaim Jubilee:

> He stood up to read, and the scroll of the prophet Isaiah was handed to him. He unrolled the scroll and found the place where it was written: "The Spirit of the Lord is on me,
> because he has anointed me
> to bring good news to the poor.
> He has sent me to proclaim release to the captives
> and recovery of sight to the blind,
> to let the oppressed go free,
> to proclaim the year of the Lord's favor."
> Then he rolled up the scroll, gave it back to the attendant, and sat down. The eyes of all in the synagogue were fixed on him. He began to say to them, "Today this scripture has been fulfilled in your hearing." *(Luke 4:16b–21)*

The currency of wellness is the state of being healthy—physically, socially, economically, ecologically, and spiritually; both within your church or ministry, as well as in your neighborhood, town or city, nation, and the earth itself, especially as the result of deliberate effort. Sustainable wellness requires a regenerative and recirculatory flow of material, human, financial, and natural resources.

Break from Usual Path

Sabbath as prescribed in the Scriptures may not be how we can take Sabbath today. So we need to find creative ways to take Sabbath. Sometimes it just means to stop and choose another path. For example,

I usually drive my car and park it at the airport when I travel. In the last few months, I have decided to take public transit instead. In order for me to do this in the Los Angeles area, I need to walk ten blocks to the Metro Station nearest me. Then I take the train to Union Station. From there, I walk over to the bus station to take the Flyaway bus to the airport. Through this trip, I see things I do not usually see when I am driving. I get to notice things in my neighborhood while walking to the Metro Station. I get to listen to interesting conversations on the train to Union Station—conversation about subjects I know nothing about, shared by people with whom I do not have contact on a daily basis. On my last trip, a young man sat next to me on a Flyaway bus. He obviously was new to the public transit system and appeared to be nervous and unsure. He shared with me that his parents decided to send him to Israel to be part of a drug-free rehabilitation program. He had tried to stay sober for five years, but had gone back to "drugging" two weeks previous. "This is my last chance," he said, "and I really want to learn more about God this time." So, we talked about the forgiveness of God. At the end of the trip, I took a picture of him and promised that I would keep him in my prayer daily while he was in Israel.

Developing the Currency of Wellness

Once we stop working and walking in our prescribed routines, how should we spend our time during Sabbath? Notice in the Deuteronomy text that male and female slaves, sons and daughters, livestock, and resident aliens are named specifically as ones who may rest on the Sabbath day. When people of different status and power roles are all asked to stop working, I believe God's intention is for us to start encountering each other as simply people, and not in our usual roles in our families, work, and society. Through the commandment to keep the Sabbath, God yearns for human community to achieve social wellness.

Covenant for Wellness

A friend gave me a gift. When I unwrapped the small package and saw what it was, everyone in the room laughed. It looked like a book with the cover title, "Commandments Sticky Notes." As I opened it, there were two pads of sticky notes—one said, "Thou Shalt Not," and the other, "Thou Shalt." My friends' laughter was for the recognition of something I do in my workshops when I talk about how we need to create a new covenant every time we form a group, so that respectful relationships can be built.

Most people think of the Ten Commandments, the popular name for an abbreviated form of the Mosaic Covenant, as a set of rules that we must follow or we will be punished. But a covenant is more than just a set of rules. It is there to uphold the well being of people in that covenanted community. For example, when Israelites, following the leadership of Moses, Aaron, and Miriam, left Egypt and crossed the Red Sea, they were saved from the Egyptians. For the first time in generations, they were a free people. In this free society, people might be afraid, since there were not yet any rules established as to how they were to live together as they journeyed in the wilderness. A newly freed Israelite might have wondered: *What if someone decides to steal my belongings or harm me when I am not watching? What will happen to me if I become old and no one takes care of me? What will happen if I end up working for someone who treats me like a slave again and makes me work every day without any time off?* Here is where the commandments (the covenant) come in. God said:

Thou shalt not steal.
Thou shalt not murder.
Thou shalt honor your father and mother.
Thou shalt remember the Sabbath day, to keep it holy.
And so on.

The covenant, even though it was made with God, was there to uphold the forming of this new and free community. By agreeing to the commandments, the people learned to respect each other by building relationships that supported each other in the difficult time ahead.

Covenants are not static; they need to be renewed, and sometimes we need to create new ones for a new context. For Christians, God made another covenant through Jesus in a different context—with all people. Again, the Jesus covenant upholds the well being of the community—love God and love your neighbor as yourself.

Understanding the role of the covenant and knowing how to assist communities to create and affirm with each other and with God are gracious leadership skills that will exchange for wellness in a community. I always begin every gathering by presenting a set of Respectful Communication Guidelines, which serve as a covenant to ensure a level of social wellness for the group. For a civic conversation in the United States, we can engage the community to have a dialogue on the meaning of rights, respect, and one's responsibilities as a citizen.[1] Based on an understanding gained from the dialogue, participants are then invited to create a community covenant.

---

[1]For full descriptions of the process called "Rights, Respect, and Responsibilities, " see Eric H. F. Law, *Inclusion* (St. Louis: Chalice Press, 2000), 120–24.

RESPECTFUL COMMUNICATION GUIDELINES

R = take RESPONSIBILITY for what you say and feel without blaming others

E = use EMPATHETIC listening

S = be SENSITIVE to differences in communication styles

P = PONDER what you hear and feel before you speak

E = EXAMINE your own assumptions and perceptions

C = keep CONFIDENTIALITY

T = TRUST ambiguity because we are NOT here to debate who is right or wrong

What is the covenant that you need to make with your family and loved ones in order for you to be socially, physically, and spiritually well? What is the covenant that your community needs to make in order for it to be sustainable? What is the covenant we need to create and affirm in order for the economy to recover, benefiting all and not just the minority who are powerful and rich? What is the covenant that the people of your nation need to renew and reform in order for the nation to be just, fair, and uphold the well being of all its citizens? What is the covenant that we need to make with the earth, so that we can continue to have a sustainable planet for future generations?

Make a Community Covenant

Invite members of your community to gather and make a wellness covenant:

1. Invite participants to imagine what their community would be like if all the resources are flowing and recirculating so that it is socially, economically, and ecologically sustainable.
2. Invite them to form small groups and write down on chart paper the elements of sustainability they have found and report back to the large group.
3. Then invite each participant to complete the sentences, In order to create such a sustainable community,
    *   I will...
    *   I will not...
4. Invite participants to share their sentences.
5. After reviewing the sentences shared by individuals, as a whole group agree on 5 to 10 sentences beginning with
    *   We will...
    *   We will not...

This list can become the draft of a covenant for sustainable community. The final version of the covenant can then be presented at worship and affirmed by all, with each other and with God.

Liturgy for Wellness

After a year of being an advocate for intercultural competency in an educational institute, the coordinating team set aside a day to reflect on their experience—a Sabbath. With the agreed-upon Respectful Communication Guidelines, they were able to share honestly with each other their experiences. It was pretty clear from the initial sharing that members of the team were emotionally tired from having to constantly endure resistance and sometimes even outright putdowns during their efforts.

As the facilitator, I decided to invite two participants who had backgrounds in counseling and liturgy to create a healing process for the group. They invited us to name those things that were destructive, energy draining, and unfaithful in the institution and to write them down on chart paper. Then on another piece of chart paper we wrote down what we would like to replace these destructive things with. We were then invited to pray by asking God to replace and transform those negative things into the constructive, faithful things that we want. After that, each person was invited to share his or her needs for the journey this coming year. Then we laid hands and prayed for each person. Afterward, the group felt spiritually rejuvenated, restored, and re-energized to continue their difficult ministry of truth-work in the coming year.

It is no accident that liturgy is always a part of Sabbath. As we encounter each other in Sabbath as children of God, and count the blessings we have received, we may also discover our lack of wellness. Liturgies help us reconnect with God and with each other as we give thanks, ask for healing, and achieve reconciliation with each other and with God. Developing a currency of wellness includes the ability to create and use liturgy to recognize the truth we have learned from each other, from the environment, and from God, and affirm and recommit ourselves to foster greater wellness in the future.

Make a Thanksgiving Liturgy

Invite members of your community to gather for a time of thanksgiving:

1. Invite participants to complete the sentences:
    • A blessing I received this past week was…
    • In remembering this blessing, I give thanks to…

2. Invite each person to share his or her sentences.
3. Invite some participants to share a physical gesture that expresses their thanksgiving. As a gesture is shared, invite the whole group to repeat the gesture, creating a kind of dance together.
4. Invite them to complete the sentence:
   • As a symbol of my thanksgiving, I promise to...
5. Invite each person to share his or her sentence.
6. End the sharing with a prayer or a song that everyone knows.

Keep the Money Flowing

Economic wellness is not about how much financial security we have for ourselves and for our church. It is not about accumulating money; it is about how money flows through our church and through us, creating blessings that sustain the wider community. One of the key ways to be part of the flow of blessings is to practice the spirit of Jubilee. Take a Sabbath and look at who owes you money; consider practicing GracEconomics[2], which can mean forgiving debts altogether or agreeing on other ways of payment using alternative currencies such as truth, relationships, time, and leadership.

Take a Sabbath to listen to the stories of the poor and powerless in your community; you might discover the imbalance of financial and other resources, causing one group to continue to suffer while others prosper. Developing your currency of wellness means making sure the financial resources do not become stagnant. Observe where resources are not flowing, and discern what your role might be in generating movement with your money and influence. Take time to discover where you can invest your money in ways that will generate healthy and equitable flows of money, achieving wellness for individuals, groups, and the community. Restoring the flow of resources might mean creating opportunities for the rich to give back, or reinvesting money back into the community where it can flow again, providing business startups, creating jobs, helping people get out of debilitating debts, and solving social problems in the community.

Sometimes, we can use our currency of relationship to invite community members to pool their resources together to support individuals, families, and organizations in need. For example, a youth center was running out of money from losing the renewal of a grant. A local church pastor and members of the congregation canvassed the

---

[2]See chapter 12 for a full description of GracEconomics.

businesses in the neighborhood and told the owners what wonderful wellness programs the youth center provided, and asked them to give their support to keep the center operating. The business owners came through with the money needed for the youth center to continue its wellness ministries.

Listen and Learn from the Earth

Developing our currency of ecological wellness requires us to listen to and learn from the earth. The earth produces everything that plants, animals, and humans need through its interconnected cycles. The earth recycles, rejuvenates, and recreates everything. The earth tells us about its health through its plants and trees, its animals' livelihood, and its water and air. We notice climate change and its consequences. Developing this currency of ecological wellness means giving the earth the rest due to it. It means engaging your community to recycle, reduce, and reuse. It means providing opportunities for people in your community to buy energy-efficient products, conserve energy at home and at work, and to make wise transportation choices. If the earth is well, then human communities, which reap our livelihood from the earth, will be well.

Waste Equals Resource—Cyclical Thinking

Alberto Sánchez noticed that the accumulation of chicken waste was becoming a major problem for the poultry industry in Costa Rica. He created a process to convert chicken poop into organic fertilizer, a product branded as Biofert. Four years later, the poultry producers, who were supplying him the chicken poop, bought him out and integrated the organic fertilizer production into their business. Aside from the ethical issue around the forced sale of his business, I want to point out that Alberto Sánchez had a different mindset about waste.[3] He saw waste as resource. He used technology to recycle what others considered waste and a problem into something useful—something of value—for the community. In other words, his approach was not linear, but cyclical.

In the book *Earth, Inc.—Using Nature's Rules to Build Sustainable Profits*, where I found Sánchez's story, author Gregory Unruh proposed that industries move away from the linear approach to production to that of a cyclical one. He contrasts the model used by industry, called the "value chain" (a term coined by Michael Porter in his 1985 book

---

[3]I got this story from Gregory Unruh, *Earth, Inc.* (Boston: Harvard Business Press, 2010), 110–11.

Competitive Advantage), with a process more akin to nature called "value cycle." Environmental scientists colloquially called the value chain a "take, make, waste" system. "The production process takes resources from the environment, makes them into products but also creates waste—including the product itself at the end of its life—and sends all this waste to the landfill."[4]

As we look at our world using this linear process today, consider the following questions:

- Who worked to extract the raw material from the earth?
- Who worked to turn these so-called low-value raw materials into so-called "high-value" products?
- Where did the waste from the production process go?
- Who bought and enjoyed these products?
- Who made money selling them?
- When these products came to the end of their lives, whose communities became the dump for these wastes?

As you consider these questions, I hope that you see the injustice that is often part of this linear value chain practice and why so many local communities are not sustainable.

In contrast, in nature "there is no linear value chain extracting resources and spewing out wastes. Within nature's value cycle, a select number of raw materials are constantly reused, never losing value. They are literally reincarnated cyclically into new beings. Nature's material assets are churned over and over in a process of never-ending propagation. And the system never stands still. It is constantly innovating and evolving to become more complex, specialized, and effective."[5]

A sustainable community thinks cyclically, emulating nature's value cycle. Materials are to be recycled and reused rather than replaced and thrown away. Waste becomes resource. In sustainable communities, people and their gifts are also to be recirculated and re-appreciated, rather than used, replaced, and thrown away.

So, where do we begin to create sustainable communities? How can we transform a world that is still dominated by the linear value chain practice, often resulting in various forms of unsustainable communities? One way to begin is to look at where and what are the wastes in your community: What do people throw away? Now, reorient your thinking to think of these wastes as resources. How can

---

[4]Ibid., xii.
[5]Ibid., xvi–xvii.

your community transform these resources into something useful for your community—or, in other words, recycle them?

From Waste to Art

Invite members of your community to take a Sabbath at the church's thrift shop. (If your church does not have one, go to one in the neighborhood.)

1. Invite participants to name the gifts they bring, such as arts-and-crafts skills, writing skills, financial knowledge, marketing skills, carpentry, sewing, etc.
2. Divide participants into teams according to their interests and gifts. For example, there might be a visual arts team, a sewing and fashion design team, a marketing team, a carpentry team, etc.
3. Invite each team to move around the thrift shop and gather material that can be reused to create something that can contribute to the wellness of the community. For example, use give-away clothes to create new fashions for kids or to refurbish old furniture that can be used or resold, etc.
4. Gather the whole group and invite each team to share the materials they collected and their ideas for recycling them.
5. After sharing ideas, invite participants, especially the ones with business and marketing skills, to explore how they can re-vision the thrift shop ministry into something even more significant in recirculating resources in your neighborhood community. For example, create an art-show event to showcase the re-creations, inviting the community to come and celebrate. Establish a recycling art school to teach young people the value and creativity in re-creating new and useful things from the things that people throw away.

Ancient-Future-Past Spirituality—
Seeing Things in God's Time

In March 2011, Japan was hit with the so-called triple disaster—first the earthquake, then the tsunami, followed by the nuclear disaster. The third of these disasters seemed to have overshadowed the strength, courage, hope, and resiliency of human communities coming together to get through the first two natural disasters. While I admired the spirit of the faceless workers who willingly put themselves in danger to contain the nuclear disaster to save others, I feared their sacrifice would not solve the long-term problem for future generations. They could only contain the disaster temporarily. As I heard about the contamination of the water and food supplies, I felt a sense of helplessness and hopelessness. This human-made crisis killed my optimism as I watched helicopters dump water into a reactor building where water levels in a cooling pool for spent fuel rods were dangerously low. "Spent fuel rods" were code words for nuclear wastes. Spent nuclear fuel rods contain fission products such as uranium-234 and neptunium-235 that emit dangerous particles and radiation. Uranium-234 has a half-life of 346,000 years! Neptunium-236 has a half-life of 154,000 years. In plain language, this means that these spent fuel rods would be emitting dangerous radiation for over 150,000+ years!

According to a March 17, 2011, *New York Times* article by Keith Bradsher and Hiroko Tabuchi, a total of 11,125 spent-fuel-rod assemblies were stored at the Fukushima Daiichi Nuclear Power Station, which was about four times as much radioactive material as in the reactor cores combined. The most disturbing fact for me was that these cooling pools were supposed to be temporary.

How shortsighted are we to keep something that dangerous for that long in a temporary storage pool of water? The U.S. Nuclear Regulatory Commission said this on its website:

> There are two acceptable storage methods for spent fuel after it is removed from the reactor core:
>
> 1.   Spent Fuel Pools—Currently, most spent nuclear fuel is safely stored in specially designed pools at individual reactor sites around the country.
> 2.   Dry Cask Storage—If pool capacity is reached, licensees may move toward use of above-ground dry storage casks.

No container or cooling system can last 150,000 years. The nature-induced human-made disaster in Japan exposed the short-term thinking that has reigned in our time. Were the short-term gains so great that we did not need to think about the well being of the next 30,000 generations? This short-term thinking was also part of what caused the financial crisis in the United States, which started in 2007 with banks only interested in short-term gains, and not the long-term well being of homebuyers. This "short-termism" had also infected the U.S. election process, with many candidates only interested in short-term wins and not the long-term sustainability of the country.

Steward Brand, author of *The Clock of the Long Now: Time and Responsibility,* wrote, "Civilization is revving itself into a pathologically short attention span. The trend might be coming from the acceleration of technology, the short-horizon perspective of market-driven economics, the next-election perspective of democracies, or the distraction of personal multitasking." He proposed a "large (think Stonehenge) mechanical clock, powered by seasonal temperature changes. It ticks once a year, bongs once a century, and the cuckoo comes out every millennium." By building the slowest computer in the world, Brand wants to challenge us to make "long-term thinking automatic and common instead of difficult and rare." He also wants to create a "Ten-Thousand Year Library," to preserve enormous amounts of knowledge from history and other long-perspective disciplines.[6]

> for a thousand years in your sight
>> are like yesterday when it is past,
>>> or like a watch in the night. *(Psalm 90:4)*

God's "now" includes at least 1,000 years in the past and 1,000 years in the future. In order to build up our currency of wellness, we need to practice this Ancient-Future-Now spirituality. We need to see the world as God sees it—the past, the present, and the future in the same view. The commandments to keep Sabbath, a sabbatical year, and Jubilee came as a result of God's long- and short-term view for the Israelites. It is a discipline of learning from the past, reaping the wisdom, knowledge, and gifts of the successes and failures of past generations, and, at the same time, imagining the well-being of future generations as we act in the present.[7] How can this Ancient-Future-Now spirituality impact our daily actions and decisions? How can we teach this as a spiritual discipline for our community today?

> But do not ignore this one fact, beloved, that with the Lord one day is like a thousand years, and a thousand years like one day. *(2 Peter 3:8)*

An Ancient-Future-Now Discipline
Before a arriving at a decision, invite people in your community to take the following steps:

---

[6]See Steward Brand, *The Clock of the Long Now* (New York: Basic Books, 1999), 1–7.
[7]Here is a quote on the term "sustainism" that also illustrates this perspective on time: "Sustainism (re-)connects the present to history and the future to the present. It's temporal perspective incorporates future generations..." See Michiel Schwarz and Joost Elffers, *Sustainism Is the New Modernism* (New York: Distributed Art Publishers, 2010).

1. Research and discover past failures and successes in addressing the issue at hand.
2. Explore and understand how communities in the past, as recorded in the Bible and in the church's traditions, have addressed this issue.
3. Engage the group in a time of analysis of these discoveries, putting them in the present context to reach a number of options to be considered.
4. Invite the group to imagine how each option may impact the well being of future generations, the community, and the earth.
5. Based on these explorations of the past and future, decide what is the best course of action.

Truth as Precursor to Wellness

The currency of truth is the primary exchange in the development of our currency of wellness. Internally, truth events serve to diagnose the wellness of the church community when members can listen and understand the diverse perspectives within the community. When there is conflict and hurt, the community can move toward healing and reconciliation. When there is a financial issue, the community can pool their resources to address it graciously together.

Externally, truth events assist the wider community to discern the truth through listening to the diverse experiences and perspectives that exist in the community. The currency of truth pushes us out of denial and helps us see the reality of our community. It enables us to hear the cry of the voiceless in our midst. If we discover that people are physically sick and children are hungry in our neighborhood, then we need to provide ministries around food and medicine that address physical wellness. If we discover that people are not talking to each other respectfully over divisive issues, then we need to facilitate social wellness events to get people to come together and relate to each other as fellow human beings. The currency of truth helps us discover where resources are not flowing and what we need to do together to restore the flow.

Infuse Wellness in Everything You Do

Here is an exercise church leaders can engage their members in to re-vision their ministries in order to incorporate wellness as part of every meeting, gathering, and event.

1. List the ministries that your church community currently provides.
2. Take each one and explore how you can incorporate elements of physical, social, spiritual, economic, and ecological wellness in it. For example, incorporate physical and spiritual wellness such as movement, silence, breathing exercises, or meditation in a meeting. During coffee hour, instead of just letting people mingle, frame a wellness question and invite people to share with each other, especially with people with whom they have not had an in-depth conversation. Covenant with each other at every gathering on how people will communicate with each other respectfully, upholding the well being of everyone. At a gathering involving food, give presentations on how the food was prepared, where the food comes from, and how the waste will be recycled. Before a final decision, explore the long-term impact on the sustainability of future generations. For vacation Bible school, the curriculum might include a segment on ecology. The children can do a project on recycling and learn why it is important to be part of the circulation of resources as children of God.
3. Make a list of doable redesigned meetings, events, and gatherings that you will implement in the coming year.
4. Create a leadership development program to train church leaders to facilitate wellness as part of every gathering.

This exercise is one the most effective ways to encourage church members to begin to think sustainability by simply adjusting the way they think about ministries—from being to *well* being for others and the earth, from accomplishing goals to fostering wellness, from short-term gain to long-term sustainability.

Wellness Events

Developing the currency of wellness means creating opportunities for people to rest, play, celebrate, give thanks, and encounter each other across class, workplace roles, societal roles, family roles, political differences. These opportunities for "Sabbath" are wellness events. A wellness event is a gathering of two or more persons to focus on one or more aspects of wellness. Here are some examples of internal wellness events: annual church community retreat focusing on at least one aspect of wellness, one-on-one pastoral counseling and spiritual directions, ongoing group spiritual direction, sabbatical plans for paid staff and volunteers, and periodic celebrations focusing on at least one aspect of wellness.

Externally, the church can mobilize its resources to provide wellness events for the wider community. Invite people in the neighborhood, town, or city to take a "Sabbath"—to rest, to celebrate the gifts they have, to explore how they can work together to ensure the flow of resources in their community and achieve wellness for all. The following are a list of possible wellness events:

1. *Health and Wellness Fair:* This can be combined with a blood drive or other health-oriented wellness programs.
2. *Disaster Preparedness Conference:* Invite neighbors, local businesses, and civic and community leaders to come and learn what to do and how to support each other in case of a disaster.
3. *Community Celebrations:* Offer your church property to the community for a cultural celebration, for block parties, for events to honor local sustainability and wellness heroes, and to give thanks for the blessings the community has shared.
4. *Community Garden:* Invite neighborhood folks to take part in the life cycle of a garden and create events to bless the harvest of the garden.
5. *Farmer's Market:* Offer educational opportunities to help participants gain a fuller understanding of how the market keeps resources circulating in the local community.
6. *Future Sustainability Fair:* This can be combined with community recycling education programs.
7. *Condo or Apartment Party:* In an urban setting, invite condo and apartment dwellers to a floor or building party sponsored by the church.
8. *Plant a Tree a Week:* Bring people together once a week to plant and dedicate a tree in the neighborhood, making it an event to learn about ecological and social wellness.
9. *Local Community Economic Summit:* Engage members of the community to explore creative ways to mobilize the flow of resources locally. The community may arrive at creative solutions to solve their economic problems, such as creating a micro-credit union, a community-enhancement fund, local healthcare initiatives that can make sure the poor have health insurance, scholarships for a sustainable future, etc.
10. *Community Dialogue Retreat:* Create opportunities for diverse folks in the community to encounter each other and share the truth of their different experiences—the rich and the poor; the

powerful and the powerless; the young and the old; people from different professions, cultural and language groups, and religions; people with different sexual orientations, etc. This wellness event could result in the creation of and commitment to a community covenant that will continue to uphold the well being of individuals and groups in the community.

11. *Take a Sabbath Day:* Invite church members to walk the neighborhood and observe what they see and hear. If appropriate, encourage them to relate to others they meet in the neighborhood as equals. Do a wellness survey. Listen to the stories of the people in the community. Regather and share what the participants discovered as to where resources are flowing well and where they are not. Create an event to feed back to the neighborhood your discovery and engage them in dialogue on how they can improve the well being of the people and the environment.

Wellness Inventory

Gather leaders of your church and take an inventory of your currency of wellness using the chart provided in Appendix A.

1. List all the wellness and sabbatical events that your church provided in the last year for the paid staff and volunteers, for the whole church membership, for the wider community, and for the environment.

2. Categorize these activities into the different wellness foci: physical, spiritual, social, economical, and ecological.

3. Explore the other currencies or blessings that these wellness activities exchange—gracious leadership, relationship, truth, time and place, money, wellness, and other blessings.

4. As you complete the inventory, what do you notice and wonder about...
   • where your strengths are?
   • where your struggles are?

5. If you were to increase your church's sustainability and missional effort,
   • What do you need to pay attention to?
   • What adjustment would you make to increase your church's ability to foster wellness internally and externally?

6. Devise a plan to further develop your church's currency of wellness for both church members and leaders, and the wider community and the environment for the coming year.

Wellness Currency Exchanges

The currency of wellness flows into all the other five currencies. When we are well physically, we can offer our time to help maintain and improve the church properties, we are able to work and make a living for our families, and we can set aside money to contribute to the church's ministry.

In a community that is well socially, we can build relationships across our differences without fear or defensiveness. We can discern the greater holistic truth that is embodied in the different people in our community, building relationships across social, economical, and political barriers.

In a community that is economically well, those who have resources will provide time and place and money for people of the community to have Sabbath—to restore, to play, to celebrate, to build relationship, to increase leadership, and, most importantly, to encounter others from different sectors of the community as children of God. When people in the wider community notice that your church is part of a constructive flow of resources and therefore creating wellness in the community, they will give willingly and generously to help meet the financial needs of the church's ministries.

In a community that is well ecologically, we understand the interconnectedness of everything in creation—the earth, the wind, the rain, the air, the plants, the animals, and humankind. If one part of the system is not well, it impacts the rest. We learn to speak the truth on behalf of the earth and mobilize our resources to restore the balance of the different cycles that make the earth sustainable for future generations.

Sabbath Empowers New Leaders

As a pastor, the church organization and I are both aware that I am entitled to a sabbatical every so often. We work really hard to make sure that the ministries continue while I am "away." Sabbatical is a way of saying that I am not indispensable and I do not own the ministry; God does. Taking time to stop and not only rest physically but also to reconnect with who I am and how I relate to others and with God is an essential part of keeping myself well so I can continue my ministry. Sabbath is also a time in which I might renew my call or discover a call to a new ministry.

The same is true for church volunteers. I have heard complaints from church volunteers that they are overworked and underappreciated, and that there is no one else who wants to do the work besides them. I also have heard from people of the same church complaining that the "old guards" refuse to let others in to share the responsibilities. By teaching Sabbath as part of the volunteer job description, all volunteers will also need to plan for their sabbatical after a period of time at the job, and take on the responsibility of mentoring others to do the job while they are resting. So Sabbatical becomes a way for keeping the leadership flowing through the organizations. Remember that wellness is about unclogging or restoring the flow of resources and, in this case, the resource is leadership.

Create a Wellness Event

Review the wellness inventory of your church. Discern where your strengths and weaknesses are. Select one area where you are lacking in wellness activities and create a wellness or Sabbath event using the following steps:

1. Give the event a neutral name and a time frame as you answer the following questions:
   - For whom is this event a Sabbath?
   - On what areas of wellness is this event focused?
2. Explore how the event:
   - Invites participants to step out of their usual roles to encounter others authentically;
   - May create a community covenant to foster social, economic, or ecological wellness;
   - Uses liturgy to help participants affirm their gifts, give thanks for blessings received, name their un-wellness, and move toward healing and reconciliation.
3. Determine what you will and will not do at this event and create a gracious invitation for people to attend.
4. Determine what resources you need in order to facilitate this event: facility, leadership, finances, etc.

Valuing Wellness as a Currency

My Hebrew Scriptures professor, Harvey Guthrie, once said in his class on the Psalms, "Thanksgiving is about remembering." To give thanks is to remember. In the biblical tradition, to give thanks to God is to remember what God has done for us. The people of Israel gave thanks by remembering how God had delivered them from the oppression of the Egyptians, from slavery to freedom, in the exodus experience. In remembering this event, they gave thanks to God by offering a sacrifice. The sacrifice of an animal was a sign, an action that symbolized this remembrance. And then by remembering and taking a symbolic action, they renewed their vows to be faithful to God.

Offer to God a sacrifice of thanksgiving,
and pay your vows to the Most High. *(Psalm 50:14)*

In Psalm 50, the psalmist sang about how God did not want our sacrifice as a hollow gesture with no meaning, leading to little action. To the psalmist, the best sacrifice we can offer is to give thanks, and this thanksgiving should move us to renewing and keeping our vows, our promises, and our covenant to God. As we remember the blessings we have received and give thanks for them, we must renew our promise to sustain each other and the earth so that the blessings will continue to flow.

Thanksgiving is the first step to enable people to notice, acknowledge, and value wellness as a currency we bring to ministries. Here are some possible ways that you can help your church to measure wellness as part of its ministry accomplishments:

Reports: The regular reports from paid staff and volunteers should include a section on wellness. For example, in a pastor's report to the church council, vestry, or session, the pastor can report what percentage of his or her time is spent on personal wellness in the form of Sabbath and sabbatical time. Also, the pastor can report time and energy spent on developing the currency of wellness, both internal and external. The report can include the number of wellness events that he or she has facilitated for people within the church membership, and with people in the wider community, such as local businesses, civic and community leaders, interfaith partners, etc.

Narrative budget: The annual budgeting process can include a section on wellness. Categorize the different programs as internal and external wellness events. The budget presentation to the congregation should also include budget items on wellness, such as programs and ministries that seek to foster wellness internally and externally.

Meeting: Build into every meeting and gathering of the church a wellness time. For example, affirm the Respectful Community Guidelines at the beginning of every meeting, plus take breaks for relaxation, meditation, personal relations, fun time, etc.

Leadership Development: In every leadership-training event, include Sabbath and sabbatical as part of every job description, whether paid or volunteer. This will also eliminate the good old complaint that there are only five people in church that do everything and they are always burned out! Sabbath will require those who are doing the job to plan on teaching and nurturing others to do the job when they go on sabbatical.

Ministry Review: In the evaluation of every event, include reflection on whether this ministry provides wellness for the people involved. Did people come away more tired and spent, or were they renewed, rejuvenated, and energized?

New Ministry Development: Include a reflection on how to build wellness events into the visioning of a new ministry, so that Sabbath and sabbatical are part of the DNA of the ministry. As part of the ministry plan, explore the long-term sustainability impact of this ministry socially, economically, and ecologically.

Worship: There is no question that spiritual wellness has to be part of every worship event. Incorporate rituals that remind worshipers of the covenant they have with each other and with God to keep blessings flowing. Liturgy and prayers for reconciliation, forgiveness, and healing are outward signs of the internal spiritual wellness gained by individuals and communities. Through prayers, name the wellness you have achieved and give thanks. Invite people to witness how they have been part of developing wellness in themselves, others, and the earth as part of their offerings.

Hope in the Midst of Un-wellness

In the winter of 2012, I finally got a chance to visit the national September 11th Memorial in New York City. Going through security reminded me of the feeling of alienation during the heightened airport security right after September 11, 2001. As a teenage immigrant in the 1970s, I used to walk freely in and out of the World Trade Center, feeling the freedom, prosperity, and promise that the United States represented. While I was feeling melancholic upon entering the park, I was surprised by smiling tourists snapping photos of themselves at the perimeters of the two giant pools marking the original locations of the two towers. Even though I was with my best friend and colleague, Lucky Lynch, I was not willing to let my emotion out, fearful that if I did, I might not be able to contain it. So, as we walked around reading the names engraved around the pools, we talked about the innocent people who died in this horrible event, noticing the diversity of their countries of origin; we talked about the courageous firefighters and policemen who gave their lives in their rescue effort; we talked about our mixed feelings about how our nation's leaders reacted to this horrible, destructive event with more destruction.

On our way out, we noticed people snapping photos of a tree—this is the famous Survivor Tree. The pear tree, with its lifeless limbs, snapped roots and blackened trunk, was discovered and freed from the piles of smoldering rubble in the plaza off the World Trade Center one month after the attack. It measured eight feet tall when it arrived in November 2001 at the Arthur Ross Nursery in Van Cortlandt Park in the Bronx, where it was nursed back to health. It was replanted at the memorial site in December 2010 and has grown to a height of about 30 feet.

I imagined the care that the people at the nursery gave to this damaged tree, working in cooperation with organic elements in nature—the earth, the sun, the water flowing through the roots, bringing nutrients to the trunk, enabling new shoots to sprout. We could have easily saved the stump, put artificial branches on it, and called it the symbol of our survival. But the organic nature of how this tree returned with life, and continued to grow, says a lot more to me about how we, as a human community, can sustain each other in desolate times.

To develop our wellness currency, we need to recognize the signs of life in the midst of a desolate social, economic, and ecological landscape. We need gracious leaders who can work together to nurture these remnants of life by putting them in an environment in which existing resources can flow through and create new shoots of hope.

Looking for Signs of Wellness

1. Invite members of your church to take a Sabbath and do a walking tour of the neighborhood.
2. Invite them to look for signs of physical, social, economic, spiritual, and ecological wellness in various forms— people working together, people sharing resources, places where people gather and connect, times when people come together and speak the truth to each other, people gardening and learning from the earth, etc.
3. Gather participants for a time of dialogue. Invite participants to share what they noticed as signs of sustainability in their community.
4. Form small groups and ask each group to select one of these signs of wellness and explore the following question: In what ways can we further nurture these signs of wellness, enabling them to flourish?
5. Invite each group to report back. As a large group, invite participants to consider the following question: What am I challenged to do as a result of this dialogue?
6. Create an action plan to foster more wellness in your neighborhood.

CHAPTER EIGHT

Reach for Wellness

I met Father Philbert Kalisa at the 2012 Clergy Conference of the Episcopal Diocese of Massachusetts. We were both speakers for the conference. I was asked to present an overview of Holy Currencies; he would speak about the ministry of REACH, of which he is the founder. The mission of REACH is:

> In response to God's calling for reconciliation (2 Corinthians 5:18), REACH Organization in Rwanda exists to serve the people of Africa in supporting their journey toward healing, reconciliation, and sustainable development.[1]

Its goal is to enhance local capacity for healing, reconciliation, and peace-building in communities deeply affected by violent conflict. I noticed Fr. Philbert meeting with the diocesan bishop the evening before the conference, a gentle and unassuming man, I thought. The next morning, he was the first speaker. I was eager to listen and learn and as always, looking to make relevant references and connections for my part of the presentation.

Fr. Philbert was born and raised in a refugee camp in Burundi where his parents had been exiled from Rwanda when Hutus began killing Tutsis there in the late 1950s. A citizen of nowhere, he managed to get permission to study in England, earning his B.A. degree in theology at Trinity College, Bristol, and became a priest of the Anglican Church. In 1995, he was able to visit his home nation, Rwanda, for the first time during the aftermath of the genocide to do research for his dissertation on the role of the Rwandan churches in promoting healing and reconciliation. He learned that dozens of his relatives had

---

[1]From the REACH USA website: *http://www.reachusa.org*

been slaughtered. In an interview that was part of the Peacebuilding Practitioners Interview Series, he said, "I also saw the great division amongst priests and other religious persons. There was no community. You could see and even smell the division, the hatred amongst them. So I left shocked at what I had seen. At that time I vowed to myself to never come back."[2] While he was writing his dissertation, he felt that God was calling him to go back to Rwanda and, in 1996, he returned and settled in Rwanda with his wife and children.

At the clergy conference in Massachusetts, he told us that the leadership of the Anglican Church in Rwanda initially rejected his effort to work through the church to foster healing and reconciliation in the communities. So, he utilized his currency of relationship developed while he was studying in the U.K., ran a fundraising campaign called REACH-UK, and was able to obtain the money he needed to move forward.

REACH now offers trainings on healing and reconciliation that are run in the form of workshops or seminars in Rwanda. Fr. Philbert said, "We bring people together that have suffered. We talk about the historical background of the conflict. There is no way one can promote reconciliation if people do not know the root causes of the hatred and conflict. In Rwanda, this hatred took its roots at least in the late 1950s so it has persisted over generations. We have to ask why this has happened. We also talk about the role of the churches during the conflict. We ask tough questions, such as: Were the churches complicit? Did they oppose the genocide? How could such a Christian country not stand up against the genocide? We then talk about reconciliation as both a political and biblical concept." In the terminology of Holy Currency, I call these "truth events" intended to develop the currency of truth and relationship.

REACH also works and trains both perpetrators and victims directly. The perpetrator and victim groups begin separately to talk about their needs, about forgiveness, about reconciliation. When the two groups are ready, they are brought together to meet and share their truth and to work on communal projects. Fr. Philbert talked about a project in which perpetrators built homes for victims' families. He described another project in which former enemies adopted each

---

[2]As part of the Peacebuilding Practitioners Interview Series, Jason Klocek interviewed Rev. Philbert Kalisa on May 25, 2009. The transcript of the interview can be found at the website of Berkeley Center for Religious Peace and World Affairs: http://berkleycenter.georgetown.edu/interviews/a-discussion-with-rev-philbert-kalisa-founder-and-director-of-reach-organisation-in-rwanda

other's children and raised them together. "Hate is a big problem. If we live with hate, we are victimized twice: the first time when we lose someone we loved, the second as we carry the burden of hatred that destroys us from within. So to be reconciled is to live together in peace and harmony."[3]

Following the training workshops, people often want to continue the healing and reconciliation work. REACH would invite them to form "unity groups," which are community-based projects that build on the different types of associations in Rwandan society, and bring together victims and perpetrators. Examples of these associations are common businesses, sports teams, and choirs. REACH helped those who had completed the Healing and Reconciliation Seminars to form many micro-enterprise businesses, such as bicycle taxi service, tailoring, handcrafts, goat rearing, and the commercial sale of milk products, soaps, and herbs. Through such activities, people not only play or earn money, but they also continue their learning about reconciliation. Through the unity groups, REACH is increasing its currencies of relationship and leadership.

Fr. Philbert described a comprehensive set of leadership programs that trained leaders and coordinating groups to facilitate these truth and relationship-restoring events. REACH eventually built the Center for Unity and Peace, located on a hill overlooking Kigali, the capital of Rwanda, as an identifiable place for promoting healing and peace building. It is an international center where people can meet, learn, and assess the methods and means needed to achieve reconciliation and unity among conflicting societies in Rwanda and beyond, particularly in the Great Lakes Region of Africa, where ethnic clashes have taken millions of lives and destroyed public and private infrastructures.

Now imagine having to get up and speak after Fr. Philbert's heart-touching, vision-expanding presentation. That was what I had to do. So, I began by taking the risk of connecting REACH with the Cycle of Blessings. I said, "REACH began with Fr. Philbert's passion for reclaiming the currency of wellness for Rwanda—social, spiritual, and economic wellness. From that passion, he spoke the truth to his friends in the U.K. and now to us, trusting that the currency of relationship that he has developed will enable money to flow toward realizing his vision. Then he began this ministry by developing trusting relationships with the people in Rwanda. He then brought former enemies together in a time and place to speak the truth to each other,

---

[3]From the same interview in the Peacebuilding Practitioners Interview Series.

achieving wellness—healing and reconciliation. From this currency of relationship, truth, and wellness, he developed gracious leadership to spread this ministry from Rwanda and beyond. Eventually, he also developed a place, the Center for Unity and Peace—a venue that will insure the implementation of REACH's long-term vision and mission." With Fr. Philbert's nods of approval, I concluded, "The reason why REACH is missional *and* sustainable is because, through Fr. Philbert's passion for wellness and his gracious leadership, all six holy currencies flow through this ministry, circulating resources and expanding and generating even more creative approaches to the ministry of healing and reconciliation."

CHAPTER NINE

Currency of Gracious Leadership

And the Word became flesh and lived among us...full of grace and truth. *(John 1:14)*

What does it mean for our leadership to be full of grace and truth? In chapter 5, Currency of Truth, I have described how to discern the truth from a Judeo-Christian perspective, noting that to discern the truth requires us to follow the way of Jesus and pattern our life after Jesus.[1] Of course, discerning the truth is intimately tied to "grace," or the writer of the Gospel according to John would not have put the two words side by side. The way to discern the truth, in which we enable people to listen and understand different perspectives and experiences, especially those who are powerless, is part of what it means to have "grace." In other words, gracious leaders know how to build relationships with and among diverse populations and to discern the truth together.

For by grace you have been saved through faith, and this is not your own doing; it is the gift of God—not the result of works, so that no one may boast. *(Ephesians 2:8–9)*

Grace is a gift. We do not work for it or earn it. Like the abundance of God's creation, we do not own it. Grace is the belief that God loves us first, and this love is not a currency to be traded or exchanged conditionally. It is something that we accept and share. In our gratefulness for this unearned love, we then have the courage to follow Jesus' way, to act and speak the truth.

---

[1]For a full exploration on the concept of what I called "divine truth," see Eric H. F. Law, *The Word at the Crossings* (St. Louis: Chalice Press, 2004), 53–74.

As recorded in the gospels, Jesus's presence in many situations created a time and a space for people to reflect and re-evaluate their values and beliefs (the woman caught in adultery [John 8:1–11], dinner at the house of Simon the Pharisee [Luke 7:36–50]); to listen to the experiences of the poor, powerless, and excluded (at the home of Simon the Leper in Bethany [Matthew 26:6–13]); to share and live the abundance (feeding of the multitudes [Matthew 14:13–21; Mark 6:31–44; Luke 9:10–17; John 6:5–15]); to share authority (calling his disciples friends [John 15:15], sending them out two by two [Mark 6:7]). These were gracious times for the people who encountered Jesus, because his motivation had always been one of love, compassion, and seeking of the truth, even when he was facing his enemies. As Jesus' presence was full of grace and truth some 2000 years ago, so should our leadership be, because we are followers of Jesus. We are to continue to be the Word incarnate through our words and action. We are to imitate his "life," discern the "truth," and walk in his gracious "way."

Love First, Not Judge First

> "I give you a new commandment, that you love one another. Just as I have loved you, you also should love one another. By this everyone will know that you are my disciples, if you have love for one another." *(John 13:34–35)*

One of my associates, Randy Stearn, created a church leadership program called "Love First." He proposes that we must follow the Great Commandment (Matthew 22:35–40), to love God and love neighbors, first before we can fulfill the Great Commission (Matthew 28:16–20), to make disciples of all nations until the end of the age. Gracious leadership is not about convincing others to believe what we believe. Gracious leaders are not preoccupied with who is right or wrong, good or bad, a sinner or a saint. We do not begin with binary, either-or thinking. We do not simply apply our rules to judge someone as right or wrong without understanding the context. This does not mean that we are not concerned with what is right. When we love first, we begin by listening to the experiences, needs, and interests of the people. We stretch the narrow space between right and wrong, and make room for the exploration of multiple contextual experiences. Gracious leaders do not see differences as a problem but welcome them and treat them as opportunities for learning more about self, others, and the issue at hand. Only after we have understood the full experiences of the people involved can we decide what is the right thing to do. Gracious leaders know how to assist a community to arrive at faithful decisions in the midst of pluralistic understandings of the issue.

Both-And Decision Process

Gather your community to experience a "both-and" approach to decision making:

1. Select an issue that your community is facing, especially an issue for which there are different points of view.
2. Invite people to form groups based on shared points of view.
3. Invite each group to describe the issue and its impact in their lives as fully as they can from their perspective.
4. Invite groups to report, without debate. Just listen and understand.
5. Invite people to return to their small groups to answer the following question together:
   Having listened and understood the various perspectives, what are we willing to be, do, or change in order to foster wellness in our community?
6. Invite each group to report.
7. Engage the community in a discussion on what is the best way to address the issue together.

Last Shall Be First

So Jesus called them and said to them, "You know that among the Gentiles those whom they recognize as their rulers lord it over them, and their great ones are tyrants over them. But it is not so among you; but whoever wishes to become great among you must be your servant, and whoever wishes to be first among you must be slave of all. For the Son of Man came not to be served but to serve, and to give his life a ransom for many." *(Mark 10:42–45)*

Gracious leadership is not about holding power over others; it is about knowing how to empower others to share their gifts and experiences and to do that which is beneficial to the community. They do not hold onto authority; rather, they share authority with those who are in the community. Gracious leaders do not ask who has the power, but instead empower the community to ask, "Whom should we empower to do what is the right thing for us?" Gracious leaders know themselves very well, especially the privilege and power associated with their backgrounds and roles. They know how to use these privileges and power, not for their own gain but for the purpose of moving the Cycle of Blessings forward.

Gracious leadership does not accept the linear, top-down, and static leadership style that assumes: "The first shall be first, and last shall be last." In this kind of leadership, the powerful are always in control and have all the influence; conversely, the powerless are always without influence and power. Instead, gracious leaders follow Jesus's circular way: "The first shall be last, and the last shall be first." Only in a circle can the first be last and the last be first. Gracious leadership is therefore reciprocal in sharing power. A leader does not lead all the time; neither does the follower always follow. Gracious leaders move in the rhythm of "lead-follow, lead-follow...," which means that a teacher is a learner, and a learner is also a teacher. Gracious leaders do not direct, but collect and summarize. They do not decide for others, but rather decide with participation of all involved. They do not impose their values, but seek to find shared meaning with others. Gracious leaders do not focus on self-interest, but on community well being.

I Have Called You Friends

> I do not call you servants any longer, because the servant does not know what the master is doing; but I have called you friends, because I have made known to you everything that I have heard from my Father. *(John 15:15)*

Gracious leaders do not withhold information, and thereby hold onto power. They do not centralize and control the flow of information. Instead, gracious leaders share information and experiences openly and freely. Furthermore, gracious leaders seek more information and understanding of the different experiences and perspectives that exist in the community. Gracious leaders avoid a narrow depiction of any issue, but instead adopt a wide-angle expanded view to see the fuller vision or truth of an issue. When dealing with new and different ideas, gracious leaders do not begin by applying the existing rules and saying, "We can't do that." Instead, they are open to exploring new ideas fully before making a judgment. They do not own and control the rules, but enable the community to accept and agree upon a set of ground rules that uphold the well being of the community.

Throughout my life, I have been blessed with gracious leaders who took it upon themselves to mentor me—Gurdon Brewster, Walter Wink and June Keener Wink, Bob Raines, Pierre Babin, Lucky Altman Lynch, and Chet Talton, just to name a few. Each one of these gracious leaders took part in nurturing me during my transformational journey—beginning as a young man lacking self-esteem, transforming into a self-assured know-it-all and even a bullish individual, and finally evolving into someone who seeks to understand others' experiences and points of view as equals, all along the way to becoming a gracious leader who can guide others and communities toward gracious transformation. Gracious leadership begets gracious leadership. It multiplies; it widens and expands and continues future formation of more leaders.

Lead Like Water

> As the rain and the snow come down from heaven, and do not return to it without watering the earth and making it bud and flourish, so that it yields seed for the sower and bread for the eater, so is my word that goes out from my mouth: It will not return to me empty, but will accomplish what I desire and achieve the purpose for which I sent it. *(Isaiah 55:10–11, NIV)*

This Isaiah text reminds us of the miracle that water performs. Water interacts with other elements—the seeds, the fertile ground, and the sun—and the plant sprouts from the seed. Stems emerge, leaves open, buds form, flowers blossom, and fruits grow large. Yet water retains its property, returning to "heaven" to be recycled for the next rain or snow. Like water, the Word of God interacts with the gifts in human communities, creating new growth and hopes. The human community is revitalized as the Word flows through it.

Gracious leaders think of their leadership role as water. They use their skills, knowledge, experiences, and disciplines to "flow" through a community, interacting and connecting different people, groups, or gifts, thereby causing new things to happen. Moreover, gracious leaders do not easily become tired and exhausted. Like water, what they put out returns to them; they recirculate their energy, time, and leadership to start a new Cycle of Blessings flowing through the community again—creating new hope, new life, new energy, new fruits, and new resources. Our world today is a desolate place—desolate in terms of our inability to build trusting relationships and speak truth respectfully, and desolate in terms of the economic imbalance. We, more than ever, need to develop gracious leaders who can reconnect and re-source a seemingly barren community, flowing through with rejuvenating spirituality, creating a time and place for life and growth.

Mutual Invitation, an inclusive small-group process I introduced in my first book, *The Wolf Shall Dwell with the Lamb,* is like water. When a leader uses it effectively, it is like adding this life-affirming "water" to the group. This "water" invites everyone to share his or her ideas, gifts, and experiences authentically. This "water" invites everyone to listen and connect, building relationships. In the invitation process, energy and authority are flowing and sharing through each person. Whenever I used this process, whether I was facilitating a Bible study or helping a group to explore an important topic, I always received more than I started with in terms of knowledge, understanding, energy, and resources. In other words, I felt sustained as a leader, and I believe the participants also felt the same.

Mutual Invitation[2]

In order to ensure that everyone who wants to share has the opportunity to speak, we will proceed in the following way:

The leader or a designated person will share first. After that person has spoken, he or she then invites another to share. Whom you invite does not need to be the person next to you. After the next person has spoken, that person is given the privilege to invite another to share.

If you have something to say but are not ready yet, say "pass for now" and then invite another to share. You will be invited again later.

If you don't want to say anything, simply say, "pass" and proceed to invite another to share. We will do this until everyone has been invited.

We invite you to listen, and not immediately respond to someone's sharing. There will be time to respond and to ask clarifying questions after everyone has had an opportunity to share.

Gracious leaders know how to generate and use Holy Currencies. We are conscious of how all the currencies flow through our personal lives. We use the Cycle of Blessings to discern which currencies are our strengths and which are our weaknesses, and seek ways to share our strengths, developing that which we are lacking. Gracious leaders also keep the Cycle of Blessings in mind to analyze how resources recirculate within the church community and in the wider neighborhood, the nation, and the world. They use their skills to build relationships and assist communities to discern the truth and discover together where currencies are not flowing. They use their skills to help people in their community discover how community members can take part in unblocking the flow of resources. Gracious leaders know how to mobilize their resources and generate movement in the Cycle of Blessing, moving their communities toward greater wellness. Gracious leaders not only regenerate and rejuvenate the currencies they spend, they also expand and develop more currencies. Gracious leaders know how to do more with less.

The currency of gracious leadership is the ability to use skills, tools, models, and processes to create gracious environment (a "Grace

---

[2]This version of Mutual Invitation has been modified slightly based on learning from using it over the years since it was first described in Eric H. F. Law, *The Wolf Shall Dwell with the Lamb* (St. Louis: Chalice Press, 1993), 79–88.

Margin") within which mutually respectful "relationships" and the discernment of the "truth" across differences can be built internally among existing members, and externally with non-members.

Grace Margin

Jesus's consistent call for us not to judge nor to wield power over others was his call for us to be gracious. To use our power to judge, often applying the laws blindly without consideration of the context, is a simplistic and lazy way of using the "law," especially when that particular law is issued by God. Jesus's way is a complex way of approaching life and relationship with others. He challenges us to treat each other as children of God without all the legal and political undercurrents that block us from truly relating to each other and discerning the truth together. To lead, full of grace and truth, means for us to avoid the simplistic legal and political maneuvers—who is right or wrong, or who has more power? A gracious leader takes time to create an environment in which people can listen to each other's points of view without judgment or power play. When different perspectives are on the table (in discerning the truth), a gracious leader invites people to decide what is the right thing to do, given what is known.

I called this gracious time and place the "Grace Margin"[3] (see diagram on page 98). Outside the Grace Margin is the "fear zone," which is the place where people can be so afraid that they will shut down, and the opportunity to learn anything new is lost. When pushed out into the fear zone, people might fight back with legal and political tactics in order to return to what they consider safety.

On the inside, the "safe" or the "comfort zone" is the place where people know the rules and the politics in the system. They do not have to think about learning anything new, because they know what is expected of them. Very often, the safe zone is not really safe, because the legal and political system can be oppressive. Yet people might be willing to live within it as long as they can follow the rules. Being in the safe zone does not allow people to explore new ideas and consider others' points of view, either. To do so might push them immediately into the fear zone.

The Grace Margin is the intentional stretched space between the safe and fear zones. This is the place where we withhold judgment and forgo power relationships temporarily, so that people can build trusting relationships across legal and political barriers, and can discern the truth together, listening to each other's perspectives. The Grace

---

[3]I first presented the concept of the Grace Margin in Eric H. F. Law, *Inclusion* (St. Louis: Chalice Press, 2000), 39–48.

Margin is particularly important to establish in order for us to be able to hear the historically voiceless and powerless.

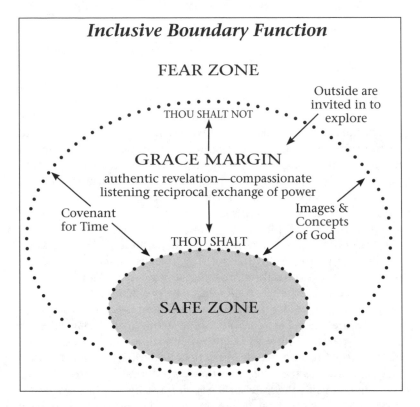

The Grace Margin does not exist effortlessly in human community. Leaving it to the world, people will go straight back to the simplistic narrow way—the legal and political. Jesus was in many situations in which there was no Grace Margin for him, nor the powerless people he encountered. Realizing how the powerful used their power to make judgment, abusing the law while so many powerless people suffered, Jesus, in each one of these situations, stretched the space between people's safe and fear zones, and created a place where the truth can be discerned.

The ability to create Grace Margins is a principal skill that a gracious leader needs to have. Again, in my book *Inclusion*, I proposed the following techniques for creating a Grace Margin:

1. *Negotiate for Time:*[4] In the world in which we live, time is often perceived as a commodity. So many people's lives

---

[4]Ibid., 49–48.

are over-programmed, and they can be very protective and sometimes stingy with their time. Yet, building trusting, respectful relationships and discerning the holistic truth require time. When there is a lack of time, most groups will instinctively move to function in legal and political ways. "Let's debate and vote on this and then go home because we do not have time to waste," they would say. Grace begins with the commitment to offer our time to be with each other. Knowing how to negotiate for the time is a crucial skill that a gracious leader needs. For example, one might say, "In order for our community to fully understand the issue with all the different experiences, passions, and perspectives, I invite us to commit to a six-hour day of dialogue with each other." If that is unrealistic, four hours could be asked for, and so on.

2. *Set Parameters:*[5] State clearly what you will and will not do with the agreed-upon time. Once you ask for time needed, it is natural for most people to ask, "What are we going to do during this time?" To create a Grace Margin, you need to know what to say in order not to push people into their fear zone and, at the same time, not to be too safe, resulting in no desire to explore. To address the fear that people might have, you need to state clearly that during that time, you will not do that which makes the people involved afraid. This will pull them back in from the fear zone. However, the danger is that people may re-enter their safe zone and lose the motivation to explore new things. So, to push them out of the safe zone, you need to say what you will do during this time that might be out of the ordinary, but important. This is an invitation to explore, to build new relationships, and to consider different understandings and perspectives; it will not be business as usual.

Gracious Invitation

Writing an invitation using the following template is an exercise you can use to engage the leaders of your community to explore ways of framing a gracious invitation to a truth, wellness, or relational event.

---

[5]Ibid., 59–66. For a full description of parameter setting in the context of a Process for Planned Change, see Eric H. F. Law, *Sacred Act, Holy Change* (St. Louis: Chalice Press, 2002), 104–110.

1. Name the event for which you are writing the gracious invitation.
2. Invite the team to take some time to imagine what the reactions might be when they ask people to come to this event. Specifically, what would be their fears or anxiety? How might these fears be expressed legally and politically?
3. Invite team members to explore what they can say to people who have anxiety about this event in order to bring them in from the fear zone by completing the sentence: We will not...
4. Invite team members to explore what they can say to push people out of their safe or comfort zones so they will come ready to explore new ideas by completing the sentence: We will...
5. Using the "We will not..." and "We will..." statements, create an invitation using the template provided.

This invitation exercise may produce an actual invitation that you can use. It also prepares leaders of the event to answer fear-based questions that people might have when doing a verbal invitation. When this is done well, it will maximize participation from the diverse populations in your community.

An Invitation to Enter a Grace Margin

You are invited to a gathering called _____
                                                    (NAME OF THE EVENT)

on _____ from _____ to _____
   (DATE)   (TIME)   (TIME)

At this gathering, we will_____

_____

_____

and we will not_____

_____

_____

(End with evoling and appropriate image of God.)

---

3. *Respectful Communication Guidelines*[6]—At the beginning of every gathering, present the Respectful Communication Guidelines (see chapter 7) and invite those present to agree to practice them so that the Grace Margin can be upheld.

Deepening the Understanding of the Respectful Communication Guidelines

At the Kaleidoscope Institute, one of the fundamental tools for creating a gracious environment is the Respectful Communication Guidelines. We present these guidelines at every gathering and invite participants to agree to uphold them for the duration for the meeting. This set of guidelines helps the community to move toward a gracious approach to sharing and receiving both information and experiences before arriving at a resolution or decision.

1. Invite members of your community to read the Respectful Communication Guidelines out loud.
2. Divide participants into seven groups. Give each group one guideline. Invite each group to discuss and write down their responses to the following questions:
   - Why is this particular guideline important for forming a respectful community?
   - In upholding this guideline, what are some concrete behavioral examples?
3. Invite each group to report.
4. Invite participants, as a large group, to consider:
   - How can a set of guidelines like this one enhance your community life?
   - When and where would be appropriate to teach and use them?

4. *Include Diverse Images of God:*[7] Notice that the last part of the gracious invitation exercise asks to evoke an image of God that supports this endeavor. Any diverse community comes with diverse relationships to God. Gracious leaders need to know how to enable people in the community to uphold and respect the different images of God that exist in the community. We are not talking about accepting all ideas of God indiscriminately. Within the Christian traditions and

---

[6]See chapter 7 for full description. This version is modified from the first version of the Respectful Communication Guidelines, which was first published in Eric H. F. Law, *The Bush Was Blazing But Not Consumed* (St. Louis: Chalice Press, 1996), 85–98.

[7]See Eric H. F. Law, *Inclusion* (St. Louis: Chalice Press, 2000), 67–82.

in the Bible alone, there are many diverse ideas of God. We simply need to know how to point to them, and invite people to explore together what this diversity means. We can raise up a diversity of God images through the prayers and songs that we choose for our gathering. One of the principal ways the Kaleidoscope Institute uses to bring the diversity of God images into the gathering is through the Kaleidoscope Bible Study process. For a group of six, this process only takes half an hour. Because it uses the inclusive process of Mutual Invitation, participants are invited to listen to each person's authentic connections with the divine story.

Kaleidoscope Bible Study Process

1. Read the Respectful Communication Guidelines and invite members of the group to affirm them for their time together.

2. Inform participants that the Bible passage will be read three times. After each reading, participants will be invited to share their reflections.

• FIRST READING

3. Invite participants to capture a word, a phrase or image when listening to the passage the first time.

4. Invite someone to read the passage.

5. Take a moment of silence for participants to capture a word, a phrase or image that stood out from the passage for them.

6. Using Mutual Invitation, invite each person to briefly share his or her word, phrase or image. (This should take no more than five minutes.)

• SECOND READING

7. Invite participants to consider the question appointed for this passage. (Facilitator should prepare ahead of time a question that is relevant to participants' context.)

8. Invite someone to read the passage a second time.

9. Take a moment of silence to reflect on the question.

10. Using Mutual Invitation, invite each person to share his or her reflection.

• THIRD READING

11. Invite participants to consider the following question while listening to the passage again. *"What does God invite you to do, be or change through this passage?"*

12. Invite someone to read the passage a third time.

13. Take a moment of silence to reflect on the questions.

14. Using Mutual Invitation, invite each person to share his or her reflection.

15. End the session with a prayer circle:

Invite participants to join hands in a circle. Invite each person to mentally complete the sentences:
I thank God today...
I ask God today...

The leader will begin by sharing his or her prayers. After he or she has shared, the leader then squeezes the hand of the person to the right. That will be the signal for the next person to pray. If the person does not want to share, he or she can simply squeeze the hand of the next person. When the pulse comes back to the leader, he or she can begin the Lord's Prayer and invite everyone to join in.

5. Finally, an effectively way to create a Grace Margin is to design each gathering as if it is a liturgy—whether it is a truth event, a relational gathering, a wellness retreat, or a regular meeting. Using elements of a recognizable pattern of worship can remind participants that everything we do in this time and place is worship—our listening and receiving from God, and our grateful responding to God.[8]

Construct a Gathering Like a Liturgy

Many liturgical denominations have recognizable patterns for different worship services. A meeting can be constructed with these same patterns. The following is an event constructed using the liturgy of the Holy Eucharist in the Episcopal and Lutheran traditions:

1. Sing a song that everyone knows.
2. Share opening prayers to bring people together.
3. State the purpose and parameters of the gathering, followed by a brief explanation and affirmation of the Respectful Communication Guidelines.
4. Study a text from the upcoming Sunday's lectionary, using the Kaleidoscope Bible Study process in small groups.
5. Engage participants in activities appropriate for the gathering (relational-, truth-, or wellness-focused), making sure that inclusive, gracious skills are employed.
6. Invite participants to offer their thanksgivings and petitions as the "prayers of the people."
7. Invite participants to make an offertory in the form of a commitment to do something to continue the work begun at this gathering.
8. End the gathering with communion and dismissal.

One can actually create a three-hour gathering using the above outline. Of course, this would also work well for a daylong retreat or dialogue process.

Developing the Currency of Gracious Leadership

Reggie McNeal, in his book *Missional Renaissance,* contrasted the difference between program-driven churches and people-development

---

[8]For a description of the liturgically based approach called "form-center leadership," see Eric H. F. Law, *The Bush Was Blazing But Not Consumed* (St. Louis: Chalice Press, 1996), 112–19.

culture. Program-driven churches are concerned about the number of people involved, attending, or participating. They are interested in recruiting people to do church services and activities. They spend their money on church needs, and staff members devote their time to managing programs.

"The people-development approach reflects an understanding that the church in its essence and highest expression is incarnational, not institutional. The new measures therefore have to center around improving lives."[9] The people-development culture begins with building relationships through which people's personal lives, as well as where they live, work, and study, are taken into account. People are raised up as leaders and released into service. A people-development church spends money on people rather than buildings and administration. Church staff spends their time on coaching people for their personal development.

To develop our currency of gracious leadership, we begin with devoting our currencies of money, time, and place for developing people. Set aside money to support church leaders to go to leadership-training events. Also, use money, time, and place to bring in resources for local leadership-training events for both church members and people in the wider community. Take time at each meeting to teach gracious leadership skills and invite participants to reflect on how and when they can use these skills effectively to create a gracious environment. The church budget should set aside money for continuing leadership education for paid staff and volunteers.

Using the currency of relationship, you can invite friends from your internal and external networks to come to leadership-development events. In addition to doing a stewardship drive for money, you should also do a stewardship drive for leadership.

The currency of truth can evoke passions from people to take up leadership. For example, whenever I have facilitated a dialogue event, inevitably a participant will come to me and ask how he or she can get more involved in this important work of truth-telling. Truth events are great platforms to invite people to continue their journey in the Cycle of Blessings by coming to leadership-training events.

As you give thanks for your wellness, invite people to recommit their time to come for leadership training so that they may share their abundance with more people. Sabbatical times are great opportunities

---

[9]Reggie McNeal, *Missional Renaissance* (San Francisco: Jossey-Bass, a Wiley imprint, 2009), 113.

for leaders to reflect on their calling, and therefore become re-energized and rejuvenated in recommitting to new leadership.

Following are some examples of how a church can develop its currency of gracious leadership.

Internally, be sure that every training program is "gracious," meaning that participants should experience grace and will know how to create Grace Margins as a result of the training. This is particularly important in selecting training programs that are required for many denominational church leaders, such as anti-racism training and anti-abuse programs. Besides training programs, we can create a mentoring and coaching system in which experienced gracious leaders can mentor new leaders. The church should also name the basic gracious leadership skill set that every leader of the church should have, and then provide a process through which leaders can receive the training.

In a world where there are not many good role models of gracious leadership, we must find ways to provide gracious leadership training for people in the wider community as well. Examples of these programs may be life-skill centers with leadership-development programs for different age groups, tutoring programs for children and youth, adult leadership-training development, and intergroup dialogue-facilitation training.

Gracious Leadership Inventory

Gather leaders of your church and take an inventory of your currency of gracious leadership using the chart provided in Appendix A.

1. List all the gracious leadership development activities that your church has done in the last year—for church leaders (both paid and volunteers), for church members, and for the neighborhood community (for example: training events, continuing education for staff, mentoring, etc.).
2. Name the gracious leaders who were nurtured through these training activities.
3. Further explore for what currencies these leadership training events were exchanged—wellness, relationship, leadership, money, time and place, or truth? What blessings did these new leaders share?
4. As you complete the inventory, what do you notice and wonder about...
   ...the strengths of your community?
   ...the struggles of your community?

5. If you were to increase your church's sustainability and missional effort, What do you need to pay attention to? What adjustment would you make to increase your church's gracious leadership capacity?
6. In what ways can you assist more leaders or members of your church to become gracious leaders?
7. Devise a plan to further develop the currency of gracious leadership in your church and the wider community in the coming year.

Gracious Leadership Currency Exchange

Gracious leadership is most valuable when it is exchanged for currencies of relationship and truth. By creating environments in which people can connect, build respectful relationship, and deepen friendships internally and externally, gracious leaders strengthen the internal network and expand the external networks of our church. The relationship networks so formed will become platforms for the community to discern the truth, which then fosters wellness in the community. Utilizing gracious leadership in everything that you do, such as one-on-one encounters, small-group gatherings, meetings, large gatherings and events, retreats, conferences, synods, annual meetings, and dialogue sessions will ensure the continuing development of people's relationships, truth, and wellness.

Gracious leadership can transform every place into a Grace Margin in which people are embraced in truth and grace. For example, when ex-gang members walk into the headquarters of Homeboy Industries, they are walking into a Grace Margin created by the staff, who practice gracious leadership. They are clear in explaining the ground rules—"No slanging, no banging, and no hanging." They are also very clear about covenanting time with them. If the ex-gang members are to participate in the training program, they have to commit to coming to "work," checking in at 8:30 a.m. and not leaving until after 5 p.m. Through this commitment of time—in most cases lasting eighteen months—they become gracious leaders themselves, both through the classes and from the mentoring done by other trainees.

When we practice gracious leadership in in our life and work, we create wellness with our families, friends, and co-workers. In our wellness, we can contribute generously to support the development of more ministries through the church. Through gracious leadership we can create community wellness by mobilizing our resources and influences to restore the flow, and in that way foster economic and social wellness. When we realize the importance of acquiring gracious leadership skills, we will be more than happy to exchange our money and time for them.

Valuing Gracious Leadership as a Currency

Worship: Commission new leaders for ministry during worship, especially after a leadership-training event. Showcase different leaders' ministries through sermon and prayer times. Offer affirmation and thanksgiving to leaders who have exercised their gracious leadership.

Reports: The regular reports from paid staff and volunteers should include continuing leadership development for themselves and the number of gracious leaders they have nurtured and trained in a given period of time. Through videos, newsletters, and other social media, create reports on how leaders have used their gracious leadership skills in families, neighborhoods, schools, and workplaces, effectively creating wellness and truth. These media can then be used in educational classes, leadership training, community events, and broadcasts (whether traditional or Internet-based).

Narrative Budget: The annual budgeting process can include a section on gracious-leadership development. Categorize the different programs as internal and external leadership events. The budget presentation to the congregation should also include budget items that support leadership development.

Meetings: Build into every meeting and gathering of the church a time for gracious-leadership development.

Membership Definition: Redefine membership to include "becoming a gracious leader" as one of the essential qualities. This may include participation in leadership training, like continuing-education requirements in other professions, as part of being a member in good standing.

Leadership Trainings: Publicize gracious-leadership-training events as major happenings, creating excitement in the church and in the neighborhood.

Ministry Review: In the evaluation of every event, include a reflection on whether the event increases the leadership capability of the people who came. Did they learn skills that can create a Grace Margin at home, at school, at work, in their civic participation, and in their social circle?

New Ministries: In the development and visioning of a new ministry, always ask: How will this ministry empower more gracious leaders in the church, and in the wider community?

The Lord GOD has given me
  the tongue of a teacher,
that I may know how to sustain
  the weary with a word.
Morning by morning God wakens—
  wakens my ear
  to listen as those who are taught. *(Isaiah 50:4)*

CHAPTER TEN

Road to Emmaus

In 2011, I was invited to give a missional ministry workshop for the clergy of the Episcopal Diocese of Iowa. At the end of the workshop, Bishop Alan Scarfe, who was born in England, invited me to accompany him for a friendly chat with Mr. Terry Waite, who happened to be giving a lecture in the area. This was the same Terry Waite who was held hostage from 1987–1991 while serving as an envoy for the Church of England to Lebanon to secure the release of four hostages. As the two British gentlemen connected, I sat back and listened.

The conversation turned to Mr. Waite sharing excitedly about a project called Emmaus U.K.,[1] a charity for formerly homeless people, of which he was the president. I had attempted to work with homeless persons during my days as the campus minister at the University of Southern California, so I knew how hard it is to find a sustainable model to support this work. As he described these Emmaus communities with vivid details, my heart was burning with excitement—this was a model that works!

Homeless persons can join one of twenty-three Emmaus communities in the U.K. In order to do so, they have to sign off of unemployment benefits and agree to participate in the life and work of the community and abide by its rules; for example, they are not to bring drugs or alcohol into the community. "Companions," as residents are known, work full-time collecting, renovating, and reselling donated furniture. The work not only supports the community financially, it also enables residents to develop life skills, rebuild their self-respect, and help others in greater need. Companions receive accommodations,

---

[1] Much of the information on Emmaus U.K. comes from its website: *http://www.emmaus.org.uk*

food, clothing, and a small weekly allowance; but, for many, the greatest benefit is a fresh start.

Waite said that he supported Emmaus fully because it did not patronize homeless people. Emmaus enables people to get back on their feet and regain their dignity as human beings. The perception of homeless people is that they are a drain on society, but the Emmaus Communities see them as resources and potential—using their time, energy, and developing skills—skills that can be planted in nurturing communities and allowed to grow, produce, and become self-sustaining.

Central to the ethos of Emmaus communities is the concept of solidarity, which takes many forms: sometimes surplus income generated from the business of the community goes toward starting new Emmaus communities; sometimes it is donated to other local charities or to disaster appeals. Companions also volunteer their time to other organizations: they clear playgrounds, cook lunch for senior citizens, drive people to and from their homes, and work in soup kitchens.

The recirculating of resources—money and human sources—not only allows the initial investment to be sustained but allows it to continue to grow and expand. Terry also shared that one of the early Emmaus communities now has an annual operating budget in the millions because people who "graduated" from that community keep giving back.

Christians recognize Emmaus as the name of a town in an Eastertide biblical story from the Gospel of Luke (24:13–32). In this story, two confused disciples, on their way to Emmaus, encounter the resurrected Jesus. They do not recognize him at first, but they invite him to stay with them in Emmaus, and, as they break bread together that night, they recognize Jesus. The whole story of Jesus suddenly made sense to them; they regained their hope, and they recalled, "Were not our hearts burning within us while he was talking to us on the road, while he was opening the scriptures to us?" (Luke 24:32).

Emmaus is not a religious organization, but communities around the world have kept the name because of its powerful message of new hope and vision, where before there had been only grief and despair. Emmaus is a movement, spanning thirty-six countries, with twenty-three communities in the U.K. alone. The organization's goals can be found in the Universal Manifesto of Emmaus International:

> Our guiding principle is one which is essential to the whole human race if there is to be any life worth living, and any true peace and happiness either for the individual or society:

Serve those worse off than yourself before yourself. Serve the
most needy first.[2]

According to the Emmaus U.K. website, the key stages in setting
up an Emmaus community are these:
1. Forming a local steering group of volunteers with a range of
    skills and backgrounds.
2. Finding out about Emmaus and how communities work.
3. Looking at local homelessness and furniture reuse provision
    to make sure that there would be demand for an Emmaus
    community.
4. Acquiring a suitable site for both the residential and business
    parts of the community.
5. Raising the money to build or convert premises and set up
    the business.
6. Recruiting the staff who will run the community.[3]

Now I know why my heart was burning when Terry was describing
the Emmaus communities. Each Emmaus community lives the Cycle
of Blessings. It begins with the currency of gracious leadership—the
steering group of volunteers who learn about the Emmaus model. As
they do the necessary research, they increase their currency of truth
by discovering the needs for such a ministry in the neighborhood.
Speaking the truth about this need, they raise the money needed
to acquire a suitable place that has both residential and business
potentials. When homeless people connect with such a community,
they enter a Grace Margin—committing their time with clearly
stated community ground rules. In this Grace Margin, they build
relationships and discover the truth about their own worth, gifts,
and dignity. They also develop life skills by sharing their work in the
community, generating income and other resources. As they stay in
this gracious place, they gradually become spiritually, financially, and
socially well. As they develop their currencies of wellness, they are
able to give back their time, leadership, and money. And the Cycle of
Blessings continues.

Terry Waite said:
Emmaus is a model for a new compassionate structure in
society. I intend to do everything in my power to help Emmaus
reach the goal of a community in every significant town or

---

[2]See http://www.emmauscambridge.org/opus25/Emmaus_information.pdf
[3]From the Emmaus UK website: http://www.emmaus.org.uk/38/setting-
up-emmaus-communities.

city. When I was released from my prison in Beirut I was very glad to be able to come home. Emmaus is home to many people who might otherwise be destitute, and is certainly worthy of your support.

At the end of the chat with Mr. Waite, he said that whenever I am in the U.K., please look him up and he would gladly show me the wonderful work of the Emmaus Communities. I am sure I will take him up on the offer.

CHAPTER ELEVEN

Currency of Time and Place

During my freshman year at Cornell University in 1974, the campus minister, the Rev. Gurdon Brewster, invited me to come to a Saturday retreat. Up to that point in my life, I only thought of a retreat as something that happened in church or in a monastery. This one was scheduled to take place at the second floor of the student union. As I arrived, I realized that this was the same room where I signed up for extra-curricular activities during registration week. This was also the same room where I auditioned for a singing group. Through Gurdon's gracious leadership, we sat in a circle to do Bible reflection, and then we did activities that challenged each one of us to share authentically our life experiences. As we moved through the day, the place became a sacred ground. I felt I was accepted for who I was, and I knew I was loved unconditionally. This retreat (Sabbath) day I spent with fellow students, staff, and faculty members was the first transformative experience I ever had. I actually made a commitment that day that I would learn how to do what Gurdon did, to create sacred places where all may have room to dwell, in which all may speak and share the truth of their lives and their relationship with God.

Four years later, before I graduated, Gurdon again invited me to a retreat at a place called Kirkridge, a retreat center in the Poconos in Pennsylvania. This was a weeklong retreat titled "Transforming Bible Studies," facilitated by Walter Wink. Gurdon said this retreat would better prepare me to go into the world after graduation. Walter invited us to engage the Holy Scriptures with challenging and insightful questions and activities. Each one of the participants shared authentically because, according to Walter, we were all experts in our connection with the text and with God. Together we experienced

113

grace and discerned the greater truth. To this day, that week I spent at Kirkridge has been the most important transformative experience I have ever had. It was during that week that I made another commitment—that I would dedicate my life to serve in this way, transforming places, and making room for others to experience grace and truth. At that time, I made the erroneous assumption that the place called Kirkridge was endowed with truth and grace and wellness. So I kept going back every chance I could, finding the time and money to attend the different retreats and programs that Kirkridge offered in the following years.

Three years later, after my first year in seminary, I decided to work as a summer intern at Kirkridge, an opportunity I believed I could not pass up. I wanted to be part of this place of grace, truth, and wellness from the inside. As I sat in meetings week after week with the directors of Kirkridge, Bob Raines and Cynthia Hirni, and with the guest resource people such as William Stringfellow, Carter Heyward, Walter Wink, June Keener-Wink, Daniel Berrigan, and John McNeill, I realized that grace, truth, and wellness did not just happen in this place, nor was it completely endowed in the place. It took lots of preparations—making sure that all participants arrived with no major difficulties, setting up ground rules for interaction at each gathering, selecting the most suitable songs to teach, employing the appropriate rituals for worship—in short, everything that would be needed from the first day to the last hour of every event. At each one of the events in which I was involved, a sacred time and place was created through the actions and words of the leaders and the activities they engaged us to do.

After the retreat participants left, I would work with other staff members to do the necessary maintenance and upgrades of the place in order to get it ready for the next group. I realized that when the place was empty, Kirkridge was just another beautiful place. It is how we prepare the place that makes it holy.

A House with Many Rooms

"In my Father's house are many rooms; if it were not so, I would have told you. I am going there to prepare a place for you. And if I go and prepare a place for you, I will come back and take you to be with me that you also may be where I am." *(John 14:2–3, NIV)*

Back in seminary, I was appointed as the seminarian in charge of the Chinese Ministry at St. Paul's Cathedral in Boston. I was frustrated that Sunday morning attendance was low because so many of the church members worked on Sunday. I started a Saturday ministry using places outside the cathedral building. Once a month, we would find our way to one of the church members' homes. One month, we would be in a housing project in a very poor section of Boston. Another month, we would be in the expensive condo of a retired couple in Cambridge. Another month, we would stuff ourselves into my tiny dormitory room at the seminary. At each one of these places, we had our rituals—fixing and eating the food together, telling our life and faith stories, engaging in Bible reflection, and praying together. With careful preparation, we blessed each other's homes with the grace and truth we brought.

> "And you know the way to the place where I am going." *(John 14:4)*

One year later, I was ordained a deacon in the Episcopal Church; my first assignment was to be the campus minister at the University of Southern California. When I arrived at the set of beautiful offices and meeting rooms at the University Religious Center, the place was empty and dusty, and obviously had not been used for a long time. I restarted the ministry by welcoming many different kinds of activities that would take place in this wonderful space: Asian Student Retreats, Korean Navigators weekly meetings, Episcopal diocesan events, different university departmental gatherings, interfaith dialogue programs, etc. On Wednesdays at noon, we had a weekly lunch ministry. At this table, students, staff, faculty, and homeless people would sit, eat, and share stories. I think we were one of the very few campus ministries that served the homeless population. Before lunch, we gathered first for Holy Eucharist. The liturgy reminded us of Jesus's graciousness in sitting with the powerless and poor of his time. This lunch ministry was like a little Sabbath in the middle of the week, where we treated each other as equals, as children of God, interacting with each other as such, full of grace and listening to the truth.

> Thomas said to him, "Lord, we do not know where you are going. How can we know the way?" Jesus answered, "I am the way, and the truth, and the life." *(John 14:5–6)*

The "house with many room" that Jesus talked about may be a place or it may not be. But I know that it is the way we take the time to prepare the places to which we have access that creates this "house with many rooms." The way is through Jesus. We follow Jesus' direction by emulating his life and discerning the truth.

So the disciples did as Jesus had directed them, and they prepared the Passover meal. *(Matthew 26:19)*

Currency of Time and Place

So many churches believe they are poor because they do not have an abundance of money. But I dare say that most churches are not poor at all. Partners for Sacred Places,[1] an organization that focuses on understanding how congregations use their assets—including their buildings—to serve the wider public, published a study in 1997 showing urban congregations on average provided over $140,000 in resources to support community-serving programs each year. In addition, the study found that four out of five of those served were not members of the congregations. In other words, churches serve as *de facto* neighborhood community centers by the way they use their place for a wide variety of programs, ranging from soup kitchens to day-care centers to job training. In 2010, Partners for Sacred Places, in collaboration with the University of Pennsylvania School of Social Policy and Practice, conducted another study of the economic impact of houses of worship using fifty assessment factors. They found that twelve Philadelphia congregations contributed $52 million in annual economic value to the city of Philadelphia, for an average of $4.3 million per congregation![2]

While Partners for Sacred Places put a monetary value on how historic church spaces are used in order to enable community leaders to value sacred places in their community and shift the way they approach community investment policy and practice, I would like to shift the way we think about time and place altogether by calling them currencies.

"Currency of place" refers to the properties from which your church/ministry operates, and other properties owned by, or which can be accessed by, your church or ministry. "Currency of time" is the paid and volunteer time that leaders and members offer to the church or ministry, often engaging the currency of place. Churches are only poor when they do not utilize these two currencies effectively and faithfully.

If a church only uses the building a few hours a week for worship and the building is locked the rest of the week, this church is not maximizing its currency of place. Because of financial shortfall, some churches rent their buildings out in exchange for money only.

---

[1]See Partners for Sacred Spaces website: *http://www.sacredplaces.org*.
[2]See article, "Determining the Halo Effects of Historic Congregations" at *http://www.sacredplaces.org/what-we-do/research-and-public-policy/halo-effect/*

While this might provide a temporary relief of the church's financial obligations, this limited way of using the currency of place will not sustain the church community in the long run, nor will this exchange help the church community to be missional.

In order to maximize the currency of place, we need to invest our currency of time (both paid and volunteer) in making the place "flow" with activities that are exchanged for other currencies, such as those of gracious leadership, relationship, truth, wellness, and eventually money.

Developing Our Currency of Time and Place

The principal currencies we use to develop our currency of time and place are money and gracious leadership. Money is used to pay for the maintenance needs and improvement of the place. Money is also used to pay for staff time—both clergy and lay employees—to maintain the place and enable ministries in it. With gracious leadership, we train people in ministry skills, who commit their time to transform the places they use into Grace Margins.

We can also use our currency of relationship to form work parties to improve and keep up the properties. The first step is to invite people to experience community, truth, and wellness in our properties, and then when it comes time to ask for time and money to support the property, people will be more than happy to contribute. Truth is the best way to help people to reprioritize their time. Currency of truth also helps us discern how to utilize the places to which we have access, and what programs to create and support.

We can also develop additional spaces in the community that can be used for ministries: church members' homes and businesses, the local mall, the public gardens, the library, the local school auditorium, art galleries, museums, restaurants, local theaters, community centers, cafés, etc. Through relationships we have developed with these external places, we may gain access to them. With gracious leadership, we can prepare and make these places into a time and place for relationship, truth, and wellness.

Learning how to covenant for time from people is key to developing our currency of time. One of the first responses one often gets from church members is that they do not have the time to invest in missional activities that might be proposed. The fact is, most people have more time than they think they have. Clay Shirky, in his book *Cognitive Surplus*, reported, "Americans watch roughly two hundred billion hours of TV every year. Even tiny subsets of this time are enormous: we spend roughly a hundred million hours every weekend just watching commercials."[3] Shirky called the free time we have "cognitive surplus." He traced the emergence of free time back to the post-World-War-II era, when the educated population ballooned and people began to work less. His analysis proposed that people did not know what to do with all this free time they had, and so they watched TV.[4] Shirky wrote, "The cognitive surplus, newly forged from previously disconnected islands of time and talent, is just raw material. To get any value out of it, we have to make it mean or do things. We, collectively, aren't just the source of the surplus; we are also the people designing its use, by our participation and by the things we expect of one another as we wrestle together with our new connectedness."[5] What if we can harness this cognitive surplus for building relationships and creating communal wellness instead of this free time being whiled away in front of TVs and other mind-distracting media?

When people say they do not have time, you can respond by comparing the investment of time for which you are asking to the time they spend on other activities such as going to a movie, playing games on the computer, or watching TV. In doing so, you are asking them to not throw away their time with mindless activities but to invest it into the Cycle of Blessings. For example, to be a host at the health fair that the church is sponsoring, a member only need to come to the orientation meeting for one hour and be at the fair the whole duration, which is three hours. You are inviting that person to give up watching four TV shows or two movies for that day so that the member will be able to participate in this new activity of building relationships with the church's neighbors.

To further develop the currency of time, you need leaders who can help church members to prioritize their time and manage their volunteer hours for ministries. In general, with people's *perceived* and *real* busy-ness, you need to covenant for a short time frame initially, with the option to buy in or out at the end of each period, paying attention to their need of Sabbath and wellness time.

Developing the currency of time is not limited to church members' volunteer hours. If you utilize your spaces to create projects that capture the passion of the people in the wider community, non-members will also offer their time to support them. For example, a church has a relationship with the local college through which students can volunteer to help at the food bank and feeding programs of the church.

---

[3]See Clay Shirky, *Cognitive Surplus* (New York, Penguin Books, 2010), 10.
[4]Ibid., 4–5.
[5]Ibid., 29.

Create a volunteer time and talent bank. Establish a volunteer job pool. Formulate a system in which people's time and talent can be matched up with the jobs that need to be done.

Time Inventory

Here is an exercise that can help you and your church members do a reality check in how they are using their currency of time:

1. Using the weekly calendar provided in Appendix A, describe as best you can how you spent your time last week. For example: going to a movie, watching TV (alone or with others), reading, walking, sleeping, working on sermon, taking care of properties, bible study group, etc.

2. Now go through the calendar again and categorize each item according to what currency was exchanged for the time, especially the currencies listed below here. In other words, how much of your time is spent in developing, or in exchange for, the following currencies:
   - Place
   - Gracious Leadership
   - Relationship
   - Truth
   - Wellness
   - Money

3. As you work through this exercise, what do you notice and wonder about...
   - where your strengths are?
   - where your struggles are?

4. If you were to increase your personal and your church's/ministry's missional effort and sustainability,
   - What do you need to pay attention to?
   - What adjustment would you make in how you spend your time?

Time and Place Currency Exchanges

How can we be good stewards of the places to which we have access? We can begin by maximizing the use of church spaces to develop our currencies of relationship. Besides using our time and place for internal relationship development, such as worship services, Bible studies, and various social, educational, and spiritual development groups, we need to expand our use of time and space to increase our currency of external relationships. For example, work with local arts communities and offer the church space for art shows, concerts, theater events, community forums, community gardens, farmers' markets, etc. These creative uses of your spaces bring members of the community to your place, and if you prepare your church members to be present and listen to the experiences and stories of those who come, you are expanding your external relationship network. Other creative ideas that came out of the many Holy Currencies workshops are to open a flower shop at the church and offer prayers when people buy flowers; or build a laundry facility for people to use for free—while they are waiting, you can engage them in conversation, listening to their stories. For churches that are renting their spaces for various non-church-run ministries, you can expand your relationship currency by offering a quarterly party for all who use the building. During these celebrations, make sure church members are trained and ready to build friendships with people from the various rental groups. You can also engage them in activities and dialogue that create ownership of the building and invite them to offer time to help maintain and improve the building.

To develop your currency of wellness, you can offer your spaces and time for counseling centers, wellness centers, food distribution centers, spiritual retreats, spiritual direction, community gardens, farmers' markets, exercise classes, meditation classes, recycling centers, senior centers, child-wellness centers, and GracEconomic restaurants or cafés. You can also offer your spaces for periodic community events such as community celebrations, health fairs, disaster preparedness conferences, local economic summits, etc.

You can also utilize external spaces in exchange for wellness. For example, you can invite people to do a nature walk to learn about the state of wellness of the earth; you can help create community festivals in the local park, library, school, or community center to bring people from various segments of the community to interact with each other. Some creative ideas include a prayer booth at the local pharmacy, letter-writing lessons at the local post office, and a wellness and healing tent at the local farmers' market.

You can exchange your time and place for currency of truth by providing regular programs on intergroup dialogue on hot topics both within the church community and in the wider neighborhood. Here are some examples: a Lenten study series on interfaith conversations, a lecture and workshop series on the economic crisis from the perspectives of the poor and middle class, and a sermon series on faith at the crossings of diversity. You can also use your spaces and time for periodic truth events for the wider community, such as community forums on local and national contemporary issues. For example, in 2012, a church community could have offered time and place for community dialogue events on the shooting of Trayvon Martin; the massacre at the movie theatre in Aurora, Colorado; presidential election campaign ethics; or the Supreme Court decision on the Affordable Healthcare Act as these events were happening to help community members to discern the truth by listening to different perspectives and experiences. Other creative ideas include a film festival focusing on a diversity of perspectives on issues such as race, sexual orientation, gender identity, economic concerns, and ecological issues. You could also present a video festival showcasing the voices of the poor and powerless in your community, and a storytelling festival inviting a diverse group of storytellers to tell stories to illuminate a specific topic.

You can also use external places in exchange for currency of truth. For example, as part of the Kaleidoscope Training Institute in Los Angeles, we take the whole class for a tour of Homeboy Industries. This ministry location, even though we did not start or operate it, becomes a place where the truth of the ex-gang members is experienced. Other examples are field trips with discussion to the local museums. In Los Angeles, we have the Museum of Tolerance, and the Japanese American Museum; both are great places to take people to discern the truth of the Holocaust and the internment of Japanese Americans during World War II.

Currency of time and place can be exchanged for gracious leadership. Internally, we use our space for leadership training programs for church members. Externally, we use our spaces to provide educational and leadership development programs for various age groups such as preschool programs, after-school enrichment programs, life-skills centers for youth, intercultural competency training, etc. We can also create leadership development events using external spaces such as schools, community centers, libraries, and parks. For example, we could work with the local schools to create a life-skills course that the church could offer on site; church members could offer gracious leadership courses at the local libraries and community centers, and, using the local parks, church leaders could create a leadership-training course for young people using the park facilities.

Finally, your currency of place and time can certainly be exchanged for the currency of money. Besides the obvious way, which is renting your properties, you can ask for donations at the end of every wellness, truth, relationship, and leadership event hosted in your church. By reminding people how they have benefited from participating in events provided in this time and place, people are more willing to offer their financial support, whether they are members of the church of not. There are, however, more creative ways to use your time and space to bring in financial revenue, such as entrepreneurial types of ministries that practice GracEconcomics.[6] For example, you could transform your place into a music and art school, flower shop, leadership-training center, or consulting services that would ask for flexible fees in return for the services and products you provide. You could also use external spaces for fundraising events, such as asking church members to offer their homes or businesses for such events, or engaging local businesses to raise money for local needs, such as scholarship programs, youth recreation center, elderly care, and so forth.

Internal-Place Inventory

Gather the leaders of your church to do an inventory of internal places:

1. Using the chart provided in Appendix A, list the internal places and locations (the church properties) to which your church/ministry has access in the first column. (If different rooms in the building are used for different purposes, list them separately.)
2. Write down the activities that took place in the last year in each location in the second column.
3. Categorize the activities according to the currencies for which they are exchanged.
   • Time
   • Gracious Leadership
   • Relationship
   • Truth
   • Wellness
   • Money
4. As you work through this exercise, what do you notice and wonder about...
   ...where your strengths are?
   ...where your struggles are?
5. If you were to increase your community's or ministry's missional effort and sustainability,
   • What do you need to pay attention to?
   • In what ways can you refocus some of the existing activities to be exchanged for other currencies?
   • What new activities would you consider doing in order to develop further all the other currencies?
6. Develop a plan to further develop the currency of place for your church and the wider community in the coming year.

---

[6]See chapter 12 for full description of GracEconomics.

External-Place Inventory

Gather the leaders of your church to do an inventory of external places:

1. Using the chart provided in Appendix A, list the external places and locations (other than the church properties) to which your church or ministry has access in the first column. For example, member's homes, local businesses, public places, schools, etc.

2. Write down the activities that took place in the last year in each location in the second column.

3. Categorize the activities according to the currencies for which they are exchanged.
   - Time
   - Gracious Leadership
   - Relationship
   - Truth
   - Wellness
   - Money

4. As you work through this exercise, what do you notice and wonder about...
   - where your strengths are?
   - where your struggles are?

5. If you were to increase your community's/ministry's missional effort and sustainability,
   - What do you need to pay attention to?
   - In what ways can you refocus some of the existing activities to be exchanged for other currencies?
   - What new places in the wider community would you consider trying to gain access to? What ministry would you offer there?

6. Develop a plan to further develop the currency of place for your church and the wider community in the coming year.

Valuing Currency of Time and Place

Worship: Create a special worship service to bless the different places of ministry, especially at the start of a new ministry. For example, one Sunday a year, parade through the properties of the church, stopping at strategic spots and inviting people to share the blessings they received in these places.

Reports: Paid and volunteer leaders' reports should include how much time is spent maintaining the facilities and how much time is spent getting more volunteer time from church members and in the community for ministries. Invite periodic reports from church members about how they have used different places to which they have access—home, workplace, community sites, and public places—for ministries. These reports can be done through video, newsletter, and social media. They can be used for worship, educational programs, and fundraising events in the church and in the community.

Narrative Budget: Most church budgets already record how much money comes in and is spent on maintenance and improvement of the facilities. But don't stop there; the budget should include how the facilities of the church are being used and the type of ministries that happened there—what blessings are bestowed through these places. For the annual budgeting process, besides having a section on facility maintenance and improvement, you should also have budget items set aside for developing more volunteer hours from church members and from the community.

Meetings: Have meetings at different places to which the church has access. At each meeting, identify the ministries that happen at these places and for what other currencies they are exchanged. At major events hosted in the church facilities, always remind people that the place they are enjoying costs money and energy to keep up, and invite folks to contribute their time and money to maintain and improve the place.

New Ministries: In the development and visioning of new ministries, always ask what kind of internal and external places are needed and what kind of time commitment is required to support this ministry. Also reflect on how this ministry increases your currency of time and place.

Missional Planning: In the annual visioning and mission-planning event, invite church members to walk through the places to which they have access (both church properties and places in the community) and imagine how these places can be Grace Margins for relationship building, truth-telling, leadership development, and creating wellness for the church and the community.

Take the Church out to the World

As part of your missional planning session, you might want to do the following exercise.

1. List the ministries that your church presently has going on in the church properties.
2. List the places (other than your church building) where people gather in the neighborhood, town, city, etc.

3. Randomly select a ministry listed in (1) and a place listed in (2). What connections can be made between the two that might create a fresh missional ministry? (Avoid the temptation to talk about bringing "them" into the church, but focus instead on "bringing the church out to the people.")
4. Imagine what this missional ministry would be like and describe it with some detail.
5. What resources (other currencies) do you need in order to realize this new ministry?

Occupy Places with Truth and Wellness

Toward the end of 2011, U.S. government leaders were attempting to remove people of the Occupy Movement from public places. These conflicts resulted in more people noticing this movement, and the truth they are trying to tell with their bodies, their tents, and their voices. Occupy Oakland was one of the places where the use of tear gas, resulting in serious injury to a veteran, became national news. I was in Oakland during that time, and decided to visit. I witnessed an assembly in progress in which the speaker spoke into a not-so-loud bullhorn speaker, and people closer to him repeated each sentence so people in the outer perimeter could hear. There were places for people to eat, to donate food and clothes, to get medical treatment, to read, to play, and to sleep. More importantly, the place they occupied became a space for dialogue among the gathered, such as curious bystanders, passionate protesters, truth-seekers, law enforcement personnel, public officials, and the media. By occupying this space, relationships—antagonistic as some of them might have been—were created where there had been none before. The Occupy Movement showed us that public places can be occupied in exchange for relationships and truth, and hopefully can lead to changes—changes that will create sustainable wellness for more people in our communities.

Around the same time in Detroit, another kind of occupy movement was happening. In places where houses were crumbling, boarded up, or missing altogether, spaces were now being occupied by community gardens and urban farms, some legal and some illegal. In an NPR radio interview, Andrew Kemp who tended a lush garden on seven city lots he owns said, "It could never happen in another city. I mean, this is ridiculous to think about this much land. There are very few houses that have another house next to them. So everybody can have at least an extra yard, you know. That's really the gift of Detroit."

The urban farmers occupied Detroit and transformed parts of this economically desolate land into places where wellness can be recreated by reconnecting with the abundance of the land.

What I admire most about the people of the Occupy Movement and the urban farmers of Detroit is their courage to take risks. Without their risk-taking, the land in Detroit would continue to be wasted, and public squares or parks would continue to be just front lawns for government and corporate buildings. If a place is not being used as a currency exchange, it becomes like a buried treasure that does not serve any purpose or good for anyone; it is just buried. In order to turn the places we occupy into currencies, we need to not be afraid to take risks, so that in these places new relationships can be built, truth can be told, wellness can be established, and leaders can be formed.

What places are you occupying these days? What currencies (leadership, relationship, truth, or wellness) can these places be exchanged for? What risks do you need to take?

Occupy my mind
With skills to tell what's true and right
So that I'm no longer blind
To the falsehood we must name and fight
The system shelters the rich
While the rest of us are down in the ditch
So, occupy and stay in my mind
In my mind

Occupy my heart
With passion for the common good
So that I will take my part
To rebuild a prosp'rous neighborhood
where justice shines like the sun
and there's food and room for everyone
So occupy and stay in my heart
In my heart

Occupy this place
With mercy, truth, and liberty
So that we'll come face to face
With our friends and with our enemies
We'll listen, speak, and share
As we learn to do what's righteous and fair
So occupy and stay in this place
In this place

CHAPTER TWELVE

GracEconomics

I notice that many church folks tend to think of stewardship of money in a linear fashion—they ask people to give money; the money is then spent to support ministries; the ministries serve people; people benefit from the ministries; the end. Sometimes, I hear people complain that those who receive these gifts do not appreciate their worth because they were free. When I ask, "Why did you not invite them to give back, which might make the ministry more sustainable?" they often respond, "We can't do that! We are a charity. We are supposed to give without expecting anything in return."

There is nothing wrong with asking for something in exchange for the services we provide. Of course, we would not expect those who have no money to give back money. However, if we do not ask, we might miss the opportunities to build relationships with those who *can* give back, not just monetarily, but with other currencies. If we don't ask for an exchange, we might be stopping the recirculation of resources that need to flow in order to cultivate a sustainable ministry.

When people ask me, "How much does it cost to have the Kaleidoscope Institute come to our church and do a workshop?" here is my answer: "I usually ask for a donation between zero and $3,000 a day." The reaction to my answer is always a puzzled silence. I would then go on to explain, "I ask our clients to contribute close to the upper end of the range so that we can provide the same services to groups and organizations that have little or no financial resources." I call this GracEconomics.

Here is the dilemma. If we don't ask for a fee, people might not value our services. But if we ask for a fixed fee, we would cut off our connections with groups that have few financial resources. GracEconomics allows us to name the value of our services, and at

127

the same time include the poor whom we want to serve as well. We would do it for free; money is not the issue. The important question is: Is this worth doing? Indeed, after I describe this approach to cost, we always enter a fruitful conversation about ministry with our clients.

Based on the old paradigm of scarcity, we would assume everyone would want our services for free! But the Kaleidoscope Institute has been using GracEconomics for our resourcing and training services for years, and not only have we been financially sustainable, we actually have a steady increase in our financial donations.

I am not the only one practicing GracEconomics these days. The rocker Jon Bon Jovi opened a restaurant called Soul Kitchen[1] (mentioned in chapter 3) near the Red Bank train station in central New Jersey. "This is not a soup kitchen," he emphasized. "You can come here with the dignity of linens and silver, and you're served a healthy, nutritious meal... There's no prices on our menu, so if you want to come and you want to make a difference, leave a $20 [bill] in the envelope on the table. If you can't afford to eat, you can bus tables, you can wait tables, you can work in the kitchen as a dishwasher or sous chef."[2]

When I read about this GracEonomic restaurant in November 2011, I started blogging and sharing about it in my lectures and workshops without having seen it or experienced it myself. So, eight months later, I was in New York City and decided to visit Soul Kitchen with a friend who had heard me talk about it in the class.

The restaurant was converted from a former auto body shop. There was a raised-bed garden in front with growing vegetables and herbs ready to be harvested by the chef. Looking through large glass windows, we could see the restaurant was full. About five or six people were waiting outside. Two women greeted us with smiles and inquired whether we knew anything about the restaurant. We explained we heard about it and wanted to find out more. The woman who volunteered as the hostess informed me that her husband and daughter were also volunteering today as a waiter and kitchen helper. She said her whole family came here once a week to support this wonderful establishment. She then explained to me that there are only four paid workers in the restaurant—Ryan, the manager; the chef, and his two assistants. The rest of the workers (I counted at least

---

[1]See the website of Soul Kitchen at *http://www.jbjsoulkitchen.org/*
[2]See article in the *Huffington Post*, "Soul Kitchen, Jon Bon Jovi's Charity Restaurant, Opens In New Jersey," by Wayne Parry, *http://www.huffingtonpost. com/2011/10/20/soul-kitchen-jon-bon-jovi_n_1021600.html*

eight people; many were in their twenties) were all volunteers. I was now even more intrigued.

As a table opened up, we were escorted into the restaurant with three other patrons and we sat together at one round table. The room was bright, clean, and beautifully decorated. Painted on the far wall of the restaurant was the manifesto of Soul Kitchen:

All are welcome at our table.
At the JBJ Soul Kitchen, a place is ready for you if you are hungry, or if you hunger to make a difference in your community. For we believe that a healthy meal can feed the soul.

Happy are the hands that feed.
Those who volunteer are guided by Soul Kitchen staff through their tasks. Volunteering at Soul Kitchen can lead to qualifying for job training.

When there is love, there is plenty.
As you will see, our menu has no prices. You select what you like and make the minimum donation. If you can afford to donate more you are helping to feed your neighbor. If you are unable to donate, an hour of volunteering pays for your meal.

Good company whets the appetite.
At Soul Kitchen, neighbors from across the street or across town, new friends, families, those in need of help, and those with help to offer come together and share a good meal and the warmth of good company.

Friendship is our daily special.
Introduce yourself to the person seated beside you or across the table. Stay awhile and stay informed of all the ways Soul Kitchen is dedicated to eliminating hunger, building relationships, and celebrating community.

End the meal with a slice of happiness.
At Soul Kitchen the main ingredient is Love, with a large helping of you.

As written on the wall, the waiters were happy and friendly and the menu had no prices. We introduced ourselves to each other at the table and began a wonderful conversation, finding out more about each person's stories. When the food came, my friend proposed that we pray together, and we held hands and gave thanks for this time and place, for fellowship and food. The food was delicious and the conversation continued.

At the end of the meal, a folder with instructions was handed to each one of us. Inside it said, "Customers pay the minimum donation or volunteer in some way to earn a voucher for a meal. Some customers do both! Please speak with your hostess to discuss volunteer opportunities. The suggested donation of $10.00 covers the cost of an adult meal, anything more helps defray the cost of someone else's meal."

My friend and I both paid $20 each. The man sitting next to us filled out the form to volunteer. I went to talk to Ryan the manager, another friendly and happy man. He seemed like a person who was looking forward to and excited about coming to work each day. He reiterated that the restaurant had only been open for eight months and people with money, and people without, were both finding this place. He told me that the restaurant was almost self-sustaining just from patrons' donations. He also said that he was writing down how this whole operation worked, once it was up and running and sustainable.

I told him about Holy Currencies and GracEconomics and showed him the graphics of the Cycle of Blessings on a bookmark. Ryan immediately got the concept and how the different currencies flow through the operation of Soul Kitchen. During our conversations, we were interrupted three times by patrons who wanted to pay *and* volunteer. At the end of the conversation, I promised to send him a copy of the book *Holy Currencies* when it is in print, and he promised to stay in touch to explore possibilities of future collaborations with the Kaleidoscope Institute in spreading GracEconomics.

Jon Bon Jovi, through his foundation, spent a year and $250,000 to create this GracEconomic business—a place where money is not the driving force for success. In this place, people find wellness in the community and the food it provides. By sitting with "strangers," the place encourages the building of relationships and sharing of the truth across economic classes. When people who have resources discover the truth about this place, they give their time and money generously to replenish that which has been spent, and the Cycle of Blessings continues.

People who practice GracEconomics play by a different set of rules, using other currencies of exchange, such as relationship, truth, leadership, and wellness. The agreement to use these currencies is like a covenant we make with each other, stating that money is not the only currency we use to value what we need or what we offer. By shifting our focus from money to other currencies, we can achieve sustainability without the constraint of money.

GracEconomics exposes money as no more than a temporary currency of exchange. GracEconomics unclutches money's hold on us and invites people to recapture the valuing process using other currencies that have been around since long before money was invented. GracEconomics helps us relearn the value of our relationships with each other as fellow human beings. It helps us reclaim the truth that if we share our resources, there will always be enough and all will be well. GracEconomics stops money from controlling the conversation about mission and ministry, and invites other currencies into a sustainability equation for building missional ministries.

CHAPTER THIRTEEN

Currency of Money

"Currency of money" is something generally accepted as a medium of exchange, a measure of value, or a means of payment. I intentionally used this simple definition for the currency of money because money is just that, no more. A dollar bill is just a piece of paper with printing on it. And, in today's digital world, money is just a number we see on the computer screen. It only has value when we exchange it for something else.

Truth about Money

Gather members of your community for a time to explore the truth about money.

1. Invite participants to pull from their wallets or pocketbooks a bill.
2. Ask them to describe the bill physically, as opposed to what it stands for. For example, it is a piece of paper, it is printed, etc.
3. Give each participant a stack of notecards. Invite each person to write down the goods and services that this bill can be exchanged for, one item per notecard.
4. Invite participants to put their bills away and start trading with each other with just the cards, which represent goods and services.
5. After a period of exchange, invite participants to share by completing the following sentences:
   I noticed...
   I wonder...

6. Invite participants, as a large group, to consider:
    *   What did you learn about the purpose of money through this activity?
    *   What can we do to recover the original purpose of money to enhance human community?

Money's Original Calling

Money was created to enhance human transactions of exchange. Before money, individuals and communities exchanged goods by bartering. But sometimes, the timing of the availability of goods did not work out perfectly. For example, if I farmed land and you hunted, bartering would work out well during harvest time. But what would happen during growing season when the harvest was not yet ready, and I still wanted meat to feed my family? So we invented money. I paid the hunter with money now in exchange for the meat and then, when harvest time came, the hunter could pay for the grain with that money. So, money is simply a temporary medium of exchange.

When we lost sight of the original purpose of money and decided to accumulate it as a commodity rather than keeping it moving as a medium of exchange, we created economic problems. Banks were created to help people manage money as a medium of exchange. For example, save some money in the bank now so that you can use it later to exchange for things you need for your children's education or your retirement. But when banks decided to "make" money, keeping more money than necessary with every transaction their customers made, the result was an economic crisis, most recently exemplified in the Great Recession of 2008.

Now, most businesses and corporations were also created to improve people's lives. For example, car companies make a product that enables people to move from place to place safely and efficiently. Markets and stores are created to be places where people can exchange goods so that they can get what they need to live healthy lives. When businesses and corporations lose sight of their original calling to enhance people's lives and decide to focus exclusively on making and keeping money, the result is economic problems.

In today's financial world, there are some entities that are actually created to be harmful to human communities. There are individuals, groups, and corporations whose sole purpose is to make money and keep it, rather than moving it as a medium of exchange. These entities have no benevolent original calling. Money is their god. When individuals, groups, and corporations hold onto money as if money itself has intrinsic value, they stop the circulation of resources, creating an imbalance. The gap between the rich and the poor becomes larger. This was what the Occupy Wall Street Movement, started in 2011, was attempting to name in their exaggerated claim of the 1 percent controlling the wealth while the 99 percent suffered.

Yet the truth about money is that it is simply a medium of exchange. The people involved in the transaction determine its value. I can choose to spend thousands of dollars to buy a paper napkin with a signature of a celebrity, or I can choose to give the same money to a charity that would exchange it for meals for thousands of children. When I exchange the money I have, I determine its value, not the other way around.

Whom Do We Serve—Money or God?

> "No servant can serve two masters. Either he will hate the one and love the other, or he will be devoted to the one and despise the other. You cannot serve both God and Money." *(Luke 16:13, NIV)*

We need to reject money as a principality and power that wants us to believe that its status is equal to if not greater than God. This does not mean we ignore the significance of money in our world today. Money is a part of our everyday flow of exchanges. To serve God means calling money back to its original calling by naming it for what it is. When we speak this truth to organizations and individuals who work with money, we are asking them to recapture their souls.

> For the love of money is a root of all kinds of evil, and in their eagerness to be rich some have wandered away from the faith and pierced themselves with many pains. *(1 Timothy 6:10)*

When You Have It, Give It Away

> Jesus looked at him and loved him. "One thing you lack," he said. "Go, sell everything you have and give to the poor, and you will have treasure in heaven. Then come, follow me." At this the man's face fell. He went away sad, because he had great wealth. *(Mark 10:21–22, NIV)*

Perhaps Jesus was asking the rich to give up their money as the first step of the journey to return to God. Jesus wanted us to recapture our spirituality of abundance that I proposed in chapter 1 of this book:

- God owns everything.

- God gives abundantly.
- We are not to keep God's resources; we are to circulate these resources.
- God's blessings are then recycled to create more blessings.

The rich man went away sad because he could not see and even imagine the fuller vision of the Cycle of Blessings. He could not see how resources would return to him once he gave them up. This invitation to give forces the rich to trust the abundance that God provides. Giving is the appropriate spiritual path for the rich toward God. It is in the rhythm of giving and receiving, living rich and living poor, that we learn to live according to God's vision of the world. So, consider it a ministry to challenge the rich to give. When the rich release their money, it can be exchanged for other currencies, mobilizing the Cycle of Blessings.

I know what it is to be in need, and I know what it is to have plenty. I have learned the secret of being content in any and every situation, whether well fed or hungry, whether living in plenty or in want. I can do all this through him who gives me strength. *(Philippians 4:12–13, NIV)*

When You Don't Have Much, Give It Away Anyway

The U.S. financial crisis that began in 2008 also impacted many local churches' financial wellness. Lower giving levels combined with declining membership pushed many churches into survival mentality. We fell into living the spirituality of scarcity. We fell into an idolatrous trap by allowing money to take control. We forgot about God's abundant blessings that will always flow. Instead of being challenged to do more with less, many decided to do less with less, just like the servant in the parable of the talents (Matthew 25:14–30) who had only one "talent." He did not take the risk of trading his resources like the other two servants. Instead he buried the money in the ground, because he was afraid (Matthew 25:25). Buried money is just paper in the ground; it has no value. When we are afraid and hold on to resources, we also stop the Cycle of Blessings. This is why the master in the parable was angry with this servant—not because he did not have as much as the others, but because he did not reinvest his resources back in the Cycle of Blessings.

So when we do not have much money, we should give it away anyway. It can be exchanged for other currencies that we need more than mere money. When we give, we interact with others and we exchange other currencies. When we give, we form trusting networks and create community. When we give, we start things moving and flowing again, recirculating different currencies through the community. This is how we stop money from playing God. This is how we learn to value relationship and truth as essential currencies that will sustain us and keep us well. When we give, we trust and serve God, from whom all blessings flow.

Developing the Currency of Money

The traditional way that most churches raise money is by asking their members to contribute. Pledging, tithing, and occasional special offerings are all part of their stewardship strategy. If we break out of the linear charity thinking about the stewardship of money, we can discover many other ways to develop this currency. Beginning with the currency of relationship, if the church has strong internal and external relationship networks, money can be mobilized to meet different ministry needs. For example, there are about 2 million baptized members of the Episcopal Church. If the Episcopal Church has trusting relationships with about half of its members, which include real communication through social and other media, it can generate $1 million if it asks each member in this network to give one dollar. If the Episcopal Church needs money to start a network of missional ministries that requires $10 million for seed money, all it needs to do is to ask for an average of $10 from half of the membership. The Episcopal Church, like all other church denominations, is not poor. It just needs to know how to build a working relational network.

Combining the currency of relationship with the currency of truth, we can broker truth events in which the poor and the rich can speak the truth in love with each other. As a result, financial wellness will flow in the direction of the poor, and spiritual wellness will flow in the direction of the rich, mobilizing the Cycle of Blessings.

Truth events can also expose the blockage of financial flow in the community and mobilize members of the community to work together to invest their money in the right places to regenerate a more ethical flow of financial exchanges. For example, sponsor a local economic summit and invite people in the community to come and learn about how money functions as part of the flow of resources. Make sure that this is done from the perspectives of the poor and middle class, and not exclusively from the perspective of the powerful and rich. In this kind of truth event, community members might discover that alone they might not be able to do much, but together they can pool their resources and create local circulatory systems that can provide jobs and medical care, and support businesses locally.

When we are able to speak the truth, representing the experiences of the powerless, the poor, and the needy, we can ignite the passion of those who have money to give. Writing a grant proposal is precisely what this is about. Grant agencies decide to give their money to the "worthy" organizations and individuals based on the truth they tell in their proposals about the needy and poor.

Combining the currencies of time, place, and gracious leadership, we can construct creative ways of using our places to bring in financial return. Entrepreneurial types of ministries that practice GracEconomics, such as Soul Kitchen, will regenerate income once up and running. Some of these ministries might be restaurants that feed the poor *and* the rich, music and art schools, art galleries, concert series, flower shops, leadership training centers, or consulting services that ask for flexible fees in return for the services they provide.

We can raise money to renovate and expand buildings if we can tell the truth about what we have and what will go on in these places. People do not give money for us to make our buildings bigger and prettier; they want to know what ministries of relationship and wellness will be carried out in those places. We can also use external spaces for fundraising, such as asking church members to offer their homes or businesses for fundraising events, or engaging local businesses to raise money for a local need, such as scholarship programs, a youth recreation center, elderly care, etc.

When all the currencies are flowing and our community is well spiritually, ecologically, and socially, money will flow as simply one of the links of exchanges. Church members will give when they realize how the church's ministries have fostered wellness for them and their families. Individuals and businesses in the wider community will give money to support the church if they realize how the church has been part of the constructive flow of resources in their neighborhood, town, and city.

Money-Exchange Inventory

1. Obtain a copy of your church or ministry budget.
2. Go through each expense item and categorize it according to the currencies that it can be exchanged for: (Time, Place, Gracious Leadership, Relationship, Truth, or Wellness.)
3. Add up the amount of money for each currency exchange and write the amounts below:

> Time: _____
>
> Place: _____
>
> Gracious Leadership: _____
>
> Relationship: _____
>
> Truth: _____
>
> Wellness: _____
>
> 4. As you work through this exercise, what do you notice and wonder about...
>   • what the strengths are?
>   • what the struggles are?
> 5. If you were to increase your church's or ministry's sustainability, what do you need to pay attention to? What adjustment would you make in how you use your money?
> 6. Reconstruct a budget format that depicts how money is distributed in exchange for the other currencies in the Cycle of Blessings. What would next year's budget looks like?

Money Currency Exchange

In most churches' budgets, the expenses section includes personnel and administration—the salaries and benefits for staff as well as the operational costs associated with keeping the doors open. The next big items are associated with the properties—utilities, insurance, maintenance, renovation, and expansion of the properties of the church. Then, for many churches, if there is money left over, they put it in programs for nurturing members (such as children's ministries, youth group, men's groups, women's groups, worship, spiritual direction) and outreach ministries (such as evangelism, social action, mission, etc.). Many churches also have debts to be paid off regularly.

Using the Cycle of Blessings, you can re-vision how the budget categories reflect the development of all the other currencies that are required for the church to be both missional and sustainable. Beginning with leadership, most churches rely on the leadership skills and talent of the paid staff to do the ministries of the church. To mobilize the Cycle of Blessings, you can set aside money for gracious-leadership training, not only for paid staff but also for volunteers. With more gracious leaders, the church can build and strengthen its internal and external relationship networks, create truth events, and foster wellness for both church members and people in the wider community. So money invested in people-development is money well spent. Invest money in staff members who can mentor more gracious leaders and manage volunteers who offer their time and talents for ministries.

You can also use your money to support local businesses that keep resources flowing locally. For example, you can use the "cash mob" concept and invite church members to spend their money to patronize a local business that provides jobs for local folks, uses local material to create their products, and is conscious of keeping the environment safe and clean. The businesses that you support with your money should also have owners who live, spend their money, and pay taxes in the neighborhood. Create a list of ethical businesses that your church members should support. When you invest your money to support local businesses that recirculate resources locally, you also develop your currencies of relationship, truth, and wellness along the way.

You can enable church members to invest their money ethically as individuals and as a community. For example, some churches give money to local not-for-profit organizations that offer wellness, truth, and relationship-building programs—such as the hospital, the local community center, advocacy groups for the poor and powerless, environmental-educational organizations, etc. In the process, relationships are built with people in their organizations, creating a trusting, working network.

Church members can also use their money to empower the voices of the powerless, therefore enabling the sharing of the truth. For example, they could invest in programs that empower the powerless—teaching them how to read and write, and share their stories through different media. Churches could supply computers and other equipment to disadvantaged groups so that they can share their experiences through social media, video projects, and documentary films.

Churches can use their money to provide wellness programs and events for church members and for the community. They can budget for paid staff and volunteer sabbaticals, plus create and sponsor wellness programs, events, and festivals: a health fair, an emergency-preparedness conference, health centers, day-care programs, exercise programs, retreats, community gardens, farmers' markets, cultural celebrations, block parties, etc.

Finally, churches can use money to bring in money. I am not talking about starting a money-making (and "money-keeping") business in church. They can invest their money in the startup of GracEconomic ministries. Churches will not necessarily make money, but they will generate circulation of money and resources in the process. Once such a ministry is up and running, it should be self-sustaining, and may even bring in additional money that can be reinvested in more GracEconomic ministries.

If a church has an endowment, it should explore creative ways of using that money, without breaking the rules, to invest in GracEconomic ministries with the expectation that the ministries will eventually replenish the funds "borrowed" in a set period of time. In other words, the church should re-envision the endowment, and create a way for it to do microfinance for new ministries.

Re-Evaluate Money as a Currency

In the previous chapters on the other five currencies, I have offered at the end of each chapter ways for churches to help their members to notice, acknowledge, and value each one of the currencies. I do not think I need to do that for the currency of money because most churches already value money as a currency. Perhaps many value money too much! So, to end this chapter, I simply invite you to re-evaluate money as a temporary currency of exchange.

- What have you learned from reading about the other currencies in the book?
- How has your learning help you put money in perspective?
- How would you evaluate the way you value money in your personal life and in ministry?
- What adjustments would you make about the way you use money as a result of reading the book thus far?
- If you come into a large sum of money now, what would you do with it?

All the believers were one in heart and mind. No one claimed that any of his possessions was his own, but they shared everything they had... There were no needy persons among them. For from time to time those who owned lands or houses sold them, brought the money from the sales and put it at the apostles' feet, and it was distributed to anyone as he had need. *(Acts 4:32, 34–35, NIV)*

CHAPTER FOURTEEN

Living the Cycle of Blessings

In 1927, a man walked out to Lake Michigan intending to throw himself into the icy waters. He was still mourning his first daughter's death, from four years before. He was jobless and broke, with a wife and a newborn daughter to support. He said to himself, "I've done the best I know how and it hasn't worked. I guess I'm just no good." He gave himself a choice: jump or think. Fortunately, he decided to think.

After a long time at the shorefront thinking, he realized that he did not have the right to kill himself. Instead, he eventually dedicated his life to "the search for the principles governing the universe and help advance the evolution of humanity in accordance with them...finding ways of doing more with less to the end that all people everywhere can have more and more."[1]

The man was R. Buckminster ("Bucky") Fuller, the famous inventor, thinker, and futurist who coined the phrase "do more with less," which I have used repeatedly in my work. After 1927, Bucky considered his life a living-experiment; he gave himself the nickname "Guinea Pig B." Part of this experiment was for him to denounce personal success and financial gain. By deciding to contribute to the well being of the earth and human communities, he believed that he would not have to worry about material and financial needs. He practiced GracEconomics in that he did not have a set fee for his speaking engagements—instead, he encouraged organizers to "pay what you can." In *Guinea Pig B*, he

---

[1]There are many accounts of Buckminster Fuller's epiphany in 1927. The best source is Buckminster Fuller, *Guinea Pig B* (Clayton, Calif. : Critical Path Publishing, 2004). I found this little bit from an MIT website: *http://web.mit. edu/invent/www/ima/samplepages/fuller.pdf*

wrote about the times when he, his family, and his work organization experienced major financial difficulties, but somehow those difficulties always resolved themselves. For 56 years until his death, he and his family were well taken care of; during that time, he had 28 patents, 42 honorary doctorates, and 28 books published.

Bucky succeeded in shifting the way he thought about himself and the earth on that decisive day in 1927. Instead of measuring his own success by selfish gain, he chose to use his gifts to contribute to the well being of humanity and the earth. He offered his gifts—especially his discerning mind—unselfishly, even when he thought he had nothing. He trusted that whatever he needed would be provided. He lived the Cycle of Blessings.

Thankfully, we do not have to go through the trauma of considering suicide to achieve this way of thinking. There are many living examples of people who are thinkers and doers of the Cycle of Blessings: I have mentioned earlier Gregory Boyle, who founded Homeboy Industries; Muhammad Yunus, who formulated Grameen Bank; Philbert Kalisa, who created REACH in Rwanda; Terry Waite, who is the president of Emmaus U.K.; and Jon Bon Jovi, who established Soul Kitchen. All of them began by discovering the truth from the perspective of the poor, the hungry, the broken, and the powerless. Instead of thinking "conventionally" about these folks whom society considered worthless—the last and the least—they put them first. They positioned themselves at the edge of society, where people and potential resources were being thrown away. They mobilized their currencies of money, time, and relationship to create places—Grace Margins—in which all people are acknowledged and valued as human beings with gifts to offer. They helped others to reinvest themselves back into the circulation of resources in the community. In the process, they turned the last around and put them first, mobilizing the Cycle of Blessings. This cyclical thinking is what makes their creations sustainable.

Rewiring Our Brains

Toward the end of a daylong Holy Currencies workshop, I was offering suggestions on how to transform a linear task-driven program into a relational-focus ministry. One participant kept responding to every suggestion with a "we can't do that" rebuttal. I noticed that this participant had arrived very late and did not do most of the exercises of the workshop. After my fifth suggestion, I finally realized that this participant has a different "brain." Her brain was wired for living with limits and scarcity.

My brain is wired to see abundance and how things flow. I see limits as opportunities for creativity. I see an unemployed person as a resource of time and energy. I see wastes as resources. I see leftovers as signs of abundance. The first place I go to when I am faced with an obstacle is not, "We can't do that," but, "What are other creative ways we can follow to do this better?" I always look for ways to do more with less.

One of the Kaleidoscope Institute Associates, Lucky Lynch, has told me on more than one occasion, "What you are trying to do in your training programs is nothing short of brain surgery." She is referring to some of the tools I have created, such as Respectful Communication Guidelines and Mutual Invitation. These tools might look simple, but when practiced regularly, they are changing the way people think. Over time, people learn to think in inclusive ways.

Nicholas Carr, in his book *The Shallows,* reported a number of experiments that demonstrated how repeated physical actions, such as learning to play a musical instrument, rewire our brains. Not only that, he also reported an experiment that demonstrated "purely mental activity can also alter our neural circuitry, sometimes in far-reaching ways."[2] The experiment, conducted by Álvaro Pascual-Leone of the National Institutes of Health, went like this:

> Pascual-Leone recruited people who had no experience playing a piano, and he taught them how to play a simple melody consisting of a short series of notes. He then split the participants into two groups. He had the members of one group practice the melody on a keyboard for two hours a day over the next five days. He had the members of the other group sit in front of a keyboard for the same amount of time but only imagine playing the song—without ever touching the keys... Pascual-Leone mapped the brain activity of all the participants before, during, and after the test. He found that people who had only imagined playing the notes exhibited precisely the same changes in their brains as those who had actually pressed the keys.[3]

It takes imagination, practice, and time to think with the Cycle of Blessings. This is why I do not like to give short speeches; I do not think short presentations can have any significant impact in transforming

[2]See Nicholas Carr, *The Shallows* (New York: W.W. Norton & Company, 2011), 32.
[3]Ibid., 22.

the way people think. Instead, I have consistently designed workshops that give opportunities for participants to repeatedly imagine and practice inclusive skills and cyclical thinking.

One of the more comprehensive models we have used is a six-month process in which we engage church teams to commit to monthly meetings. Each meeting is at least five hours long, and, in-between meetings, participants have assignments through which they can practice what they have learned. At the end of one of these trainings with teams from sixteen churches, participants shared new missional and sustainable ideas for ministries. Some of these ideas were pretty "far out" for most churches. For example, one church team was considering starting a ministry at the bail-bonds–service agency in town. They said, "We spend a lot of time and money training missionaries to go overseas; why aren't we spending the same amount of energy, time, and money training people to do missional work right in our backyard. People who go to the bail-bond office are in some kind of trouble, and we can do something about that."

I asked the people in the workshop, "If I had presented this idea to you six months ago, would you have even considered it?"
"No!" They responded loudly.
"Then what happened?" I asked, "Why are you not afraid of these ideas?"
"You have successfully rewired our brains!" one participant shouted out, and everyone applauded.

I have heard the term "paradigm shift" applied to church transformations for over thirty years. Yet, there are very few resources that actually help people and communities to shift their paradigms—rewire their brains. My hope in writing this book is to enable the readers to achieve real paradigm shifts—from internal to external focus, from holding on to letting go, from resources being static to flowing, from stagnation to circulation, from doing to relating, from holding onto power to sharing blessings, from fear to grace, from maintenance to mission.

To attempt to achieve this shift with my readers, I use repetition. You might have noticed that I revisited all the currencies in the Cycle of Blessings in every chapter. There were ideas that were shared in one chapter; they were then repeated in another chapter when I talked about another currency. This means that these currencies are all related and connected in how they flow into each other. Through repetition, I invite readers to imagine again and again what living the Cycle of Blessings is like.

I also proposed many activities (in boxes throughout each chapter) that you can do yourselves and with people in your community. By practicing processes that embody different parts of the Cycle of Blessings, you and your community might actually move toward rewiring your brains to think missionally and sustainably. If you have not done any of these activities, I invite you to go back to do them. Remember that you need to practice repeatedly over time in order to accomplish the shift in paradigm.

Finally, the limit of the printed page is that it is linear. There is the beginning and the end of the book. However, you do not have to read this book in a linear fashion. Now that you are almost at the end of the book, you might want to practice cyclical thinking and go back and reread a previous chapter and re-enact another exercise. You do not have to follow the order of information and activities I have presented; feel free to move from one currency to another, following your interest.

Ways to Embrace the Cycle of Blessings

As you review your learning and experience of the Holy Currencies and how they flow through the Cycle of Blessings, here are some areas of application I invite you to consider:

1. *Personal Spirituality*: As a leader, apply the Cycle of Blessings to your life and ministry. Do the "Time Inventory" exercise in chapter 11 and explore how you have apportioned your time for the different currencies. Which currencies do you have and value, and which currencies are you lacking and in need of development? How would you adjust your thinking and what would you do in order to develop these currencies? Create a personal action plan based on this reflection.

2. *Congregation Vitality Assessment*: Working with leaders of your church, do all the inventory exercises in Appendix A. Discern which currencies are your strengths and which are your weaknesses. Do you have a balance of internal and external movements in relationship, truth, wellness, and leadership? What would you do and how would you adjust your thinking in order to develop those currencies in which you are lacking? Create a six-month action plan based on this exploration.

3. *Assessment of the Flow of Resources in the Wider Community*: Using the Cycle of Blessings, you can analyze how resources are circulating in the wider community. What are the signs of blessing flowing through your community? How can you

help people in your community acknowledge and celebrate these blessings? Where do the currencies become stagnated? How can your church take part in unclogging the blockage? How can you mobilize the currencies that your church has to restore the healthy circulation of resources? How can your church be a place where blessings flow in and out, rejuvenating the wider community?

4. *Change the Way Your Church Values Currencies*: Working with leaders of your church, review the various ways to value the various Holy Currencies, described at the end of chapters 3, 5, 7, 9 and 11. Explore which of these suggestions can be implemented to help members of your community recognize and affirm the flowing of these currencies toward blessings internally for church members and externally for the wider community.

5. *Redesign Worship*: You can use the Cycle of Blessings to design a liturgy. Worship begins with people taking their time to come to a place. How do you use gracious leadership to enable worshipers to build stronger relationships? How does the liturgy enable participants to speak and listen to the truth through sermon, music, prayers, and other kinds of presentations? Where in the liturgy does it foster spiritual wellness? If your worship indeed provides relationship, truth, and wellness, worshipers will be happy to contribute money and time to support the ministry of the church, which in part will enhance the leadership capability and maintenance and improvement of properties of your church.

6. *Redesign Gatherings*: Keeping the Cycle of Blessings in mind, you can redesign an annual conference, convention, synod, assembly, or local and regional gathering, making sure that all six currencies are flowing. Again, start with a time and a place for these gatherings. What part of the agenda builds relationships, speaks the truth, fosters wellness, increases gracious leadership, and strengthens financial stewardship? Decide how these differently focused agenda items should flow, and create a comprehensive agenda.

7. *Re-Envision an Existing Ministry*: You can use the Cycle of Blessings to analyze an existing ministry and see what you need to do to make it sustainable and missional. Sometimes, it is just a readjustment of the way people think about that ministry that will transform it. Invite the leaders of the ministry to work through the following exercises: "From Task

to Relationship"(chapter 3), "Add Truth to Everything You Do" (chapter 5), and "Infuse Wellness in Everything You Do" (chapter 7). Because the currencies of relationship, truth, and wellness are often lacking in many ministries, redesigning a ministry based on the reflections from these exercises will expand the flow of these currencies, creating a more complete Cycle of Blessings, which will make the ministry missional and sustainable.

8. *Incubate a New Ministry*: To create a new ministry, you can start anywhere in the Cycle of Blessings and imagine how each of the currencies can flow and rejuvenate each other. Ask at the end of the reflection: *What is God calling you to do?* Create a ministry plan that will incorporate all the currencies of the Cycle of Blessings:

   a. Name the truth you are seeking and the wellness you are fostering in this new ministry;

   b. Construct a relational network that supports this ministry;

   c. Establish a place and time in which this ministry will take place;

   d. Create a wellness plan for people involved;

   e. Develop a leadership-training process to empower people for this ministry;

   f. Find initial investors to give money, time, and talent to launch this ministry;

   g. Formulate a financial plan for ongoing financial sustainability, perhaps using GracEconomics; and

   h. Project a time frame when this ministry will be self-sustaining.

How Are the Currencies Flowing in Your Ministry?

1. Make a list of ministries in which you are presently engaged.

2. Select one ministry of which you have the most knowledge—its mission, finances, organizing, populations served, etc.

3. Using the worksheet provided in Appendix B, in and around each one of the boxes representing one of the currencies that this ministry currently possesses, write down as many items as you can think of. If you are working on this with others serving in the same ministry, feel free to have discussions with them.

4.   Remembering that these currencies are of little value unless they are exchanged for or flow into blessings or other currencies, draw arrows representing how these currencies are currently flowing. For example, given the budget this ministry has (money), part of it goes to maintaining the building and salary for the staff, so put an arrow from "money" to "time and place." If your ministry has a budget item for gracious-leadership training, then put an arrow from "money" to "gracious leadership." To give another example, a church currently has significant relationships with civic and community leaders by hosting a monthly community-wellness meeting in the church building. For this, that church would put two arrows coming from "time and place": one going to "relationship," and the other going to "wellness."

5.   As you work though this exercise, what do you notice and wonder about...
   • where the strengths of the ministry are?
   • where the weaknesses are?
If you were to maximize the Cycle of Blessings for this ministry, making it missional and sustainable,
   • What do you need to pay attention to?
   • In what ways can you refocus some of the existing activities?
   • What new activities would you consider doing?

6.   Redesign a ministry plan for the coming year, incorporating all the currencies of the Cycle of Blessings.

Appendix A

Currencies Inventory of Your Church

Currency of Relationship Inventory

Currency of Relationship: Refers to the internal and external networks of mutually respectful connections that leaders and members of a church or ministry have. Internal connections include constructive relationships among members and leaders, area churches or ministries of the same affiliation, area denominational organizations, and national and international denominational structures. External connections include constructive relationships with non-members, different racial, cultural and ethnic groups in the neighborhood, people with resources and people in need in the community, civic community leaders, ecumenical and interfaith partners, community and civic organizations, and local businesses.

Instructions:

Gather leaders of your church and take an inventory of the internal and external relationships of your church using Tables I and II at end of inventory.

Internal Relationship Inventory (Table I):

1. Name the key persons or groups who have been involved in building relationships in your internal network, whether among church members, area churches, area denominational organizations, or national and international denominational structures.
2. Rate these relationships: None – weak – okay – strong
3. For what currencies and other blessings can these relationships exchanged

External Relationship Inventory (Table II):

1. Name the key persons or groups who have been involved in building relationships for your external network: with

people not already members; with different racial, cultural, and ethnic groups in the neighborhood; with individuals and groups with resources, or individuals and groups in need; or with civic and community leaders, ecumenical and interfaith partners, local businesses, civic and community organizations, and environmental groups.
2. Rate these relationships: None – weak – okay – strong
3. For what currencies and other blessings can these relationships be exchanged?

For the visual learners, draw a network map of your church or ministry based on the completed inventories of internal and external relationships. Draw a big circle on a piece of paper. Put the internal network inside the circle and the external network outside the circle. Draw lines to represent the connections between the key people and groups.

1. As you work through the two exercises, what do you notice and wonder about...
   ...where your strengths lie?
   ...where your struggles occur?
2. If you were to increase your ministry's missional effort and its sustainability:
   What do you need to pay attention to?
   What adjustment would you make to increase the effectiveness of your network, both internal and external?
3. In what ways can you assist the leaders and members of your church or ministry to increase the effectiveness of their ministry network, whether internal or external?

Develop a plan to continue to strengthen existing relationships by building up the capacity of the internal network. More importantly, develop a plan to enable church members to build mutually respectful external relationships in the areas where you are deficient.

Table I: Internal Currency of Relationship Inventory

Internal relationships	Name the key people or groups involved in building these relationships	Rate these relationships: (none, weak, okay, strong)	Currencies exchange: Gracious Leadership Truth Time and Place Money Wellness Relationship Other Blessings
Among members			
Among area churches of the same affiliation			
With area denominational organization			
With national denominational structure			

Table II: External Currency of Relationship Inventory

External relationships: with people not already members of the church	Name the key people or groups involved in building these relationships	Rate these relationships: (none, weak, okay, strong)	Currencies exchange: Gracious Leadership Truth Time and Place Money Wellness Relationship Other Blessings
Different racial, cultural, and ethnic groups in the neighborhood			
Individuals and groups with resources			
Individuals and groups in need			
Civic and community leaders			
Ecumenical and interfaith partners			
Local businesses			
Civic and community organizations			
Environment			

Currency of Truth Inventory

Currency of Truth: It is the ability to articulate individually and corporately the global and wholistic truth, both internally—the experiences of different individuals and groups within the church or ministry—and externally—the experiences of different individuals and groups in the community, the neighborhood, the town or city, the nation, and the earth.

Instructions:

Gather leaders of your church and take an inventory of your currency of truth using Table III.

1. Internally, what has your church done in the last year to enable church members to discern the truth? In what ways has your church engaged members to dialogue and understand the different perspectives on internal issues, especially in decision-making process?

2. Externally, what has your church done in the last year to assist the wider community—neighborhood, town, or city—to discern the truth, especially when the community was facing issues of impact? In what ways has your church provided opportunities (truth events) for members of the wider community to dialogue and achieve understanding of the different perspectives of community issues, moving toward the possibility of a constructive and faithful resolution? These issues might be on immigration, sexual orientation, political debates, economic injustice, interfaith concerns, interracial tension, environmental concerns, etc. What has your church done to enable the people of your community to listen to the earth and discern the truth about the environment?

3. Make a list of the "truth events" that your church has facilitated in the last year.

4. Further explore for which currencies these truth events exchanged—wellness, relationship, leadership, money, time and place or truth? Remember that it is the exchange of these currencies that give them value.

5. As you complete the inventory, what do you notice and wonder about...
   • where your strengths are?
   • where your struggles are?

6. If you were to increase your church's sustainability and missional effort:
   • What do you need to pay attention to?
   • What adjustment would you make to increase your church's ability to discern the truth internally and externally?
7. In what ways can you assist the leaders and members of your church to increase their ability to be truth-seeking people?
8. Develop a plan to further develop your church's currency of truth, addressing internal and external issues in the coming year.

Table III: Currency of Truth Inventory

	List "Truth Events" facilitated in the last year	Currencies exchange: Gracious Leadership Relationship Time and Place Money Wellness Truth Other Blessings
Internal: Among church members		
External: For the neighborhood		
External: For the city or state		
External: For the environment		

Currency of Wellness Inventory

Currency of Wellness: This is the state of being healthy physically, socially, economically, ecologically, and spiritually within a church or ministry, the neighborhood, the town or city, nation, or the earth, especially as the result of deliberate effort. Sustainable wellness requires regenerative and circulatory flow of material, human, financial, and natural resources.

Instructions:

Gather leaders of your church and take an inventory of your currency of wellness using Table IV.

1. List all the wellness and sabbatical events or activities that your church provided in the last year for the paid staff and volunteers, for the whole church membership, for the wider community, or for the environment.
2. Categorize these activities into the different wellness foci: physical, spiritual, social, economical, and ecological.
3. Explore for what other currencies or blessings these wellness activities were exchanged: gracious leadership, relationship, truth, time and place, money, wellness or other blessings.
4. As you complete the inventory, what do you notice and wonder about...
   • where your strengths are?
   • where your struggles are?
5. If you were to increase your church's sustainability and missional effort:
   • What do you need to pay attention to?
   • What adjustment would you make to increase your church's ability to foster wellness internally and externally?
6. Develop a plan to further develop your church's currency of wellness for both church members and leaders, and the wider community and the environment for the coming year.

Table IV: Currency of Wellness Inventory

	List wellness and sabbatical activities	Categorize these activities: Spiritual Wellness Physical Wellness Social Wellness Ecological Wellness Economical Wellness	Currencies exchange: Gracious Leadership Relationship Truth Time and Place Money Wellness Other Blessings
Church leaders			
Church members			
Neighborhood folks			
The environment			

Currency of Gracious Leadership Inventory

Currency of Gracious Leadership: It is the ability to use skills, tools, models, and processes to create gracious environments (Grace Margins) within which mutually respectful "relationships" and the discernment of the "truth" across differences can be built internally, among existing members, and externally, with non-members. Differences can be racial/ ethnic, age, gender, sexual orientation, class, political affiliation, or just between church members and folks in the neighborhood.

Instructions:

Gather leaders of your church and take an inventory of your currency of gracious leadership using Table V.

1. List all the gracious leadership development activities that your church has done in the last year: for church leaders (both paid and volunteers), for church members, and for the neighborhood community (for example: training events, continuing education for staff, mentoring, etc.).
2. Name the gracious leaders who were nurtured through these training activities.
3. Further explore for what currencies these leadership training events were exchanged: wellness, relationship, leadership, money, time and place, or truth? What blessings did these new leaders share?
4. As you complete the inventory, what do you notice and wonder about…
   the strengths of your community?
   the struggles of your community?
5. If you were to increase your church's sustainability and missional effort:
   • What do you need to pay attention to?
   • What adjustment would you make to increase your church's gracious leadership capacity?
6. In what ways can you assist more leaders or members of your church to become gracious leaders?
7. Develop a plan to further develop the currency of gracious leadership in your church and the wider community in the coming year.

Table V: Currency of Gracious Leadership Inventory

	List gracious leadership development activities in the last year	Name the gracious leaders nurtured through these activities	Currencies exchange: Relationship Truth Time and Place Money Wellness Gracious Leadership Other Blessings
Church leaders			
Church members			
Neighborhood folks			
Others			

Currency of Time Inventory

Currency of Time: Refers to paid and volunteer time that leaders and members offer to the church or ministry.

Instructions:

Gather leaders of your church members do an inventory of their currency of time using Table VI: (This inventory exercise can also be done individually for personal reflection on how you distribute your time for the different currencies in the Cycle of Blessings)

1. Using the weekly calendar provided in Table VI, describe to the best of your abilities how you spent your time last week. For example, going to a movie, watching TV (alone or with others), reading, walking, sleeping, working on sermon, taking care of properties, bible study group, etc.

2. Now go through the calendar again and categorize each item according to what currency was exchanged for the time, especially the currencies listed below here. In other words, how much of your time is spent in developing, or being exchanged for, the following currencies:
   - Place
   - Gracious Leadership
   - Relationship
   - Truth
   - Wellness
   - Money

3. As you work through this exercise, what do you notice and wonder about...
   - where your strengths are?
   - where your struggles are?

4. Invite participants to share their reflections.

5. If you were to increase your personal and your church or ministry's missional effort and sustainability:
   - What do you need to pay attention to?
   - What adjustment would you make in how you spend your time?

Table VI: Currency of Time Inventory

	Sun	Mon	Tue	Wed	Thur	Fri	Sat
5 am :30							
6 am :30							
7 am :30							
8 am :30							
9 am :30							
10 am :30							
11 am :30							
12 pm :30							
1 pm :30							
2 pm :30							
3 pm :30							
4 pm :30							
5 pm :30							
6 pm :30							
7 pm :30							
8 pm :30							
9 pm :30							
10 pm :30							
11 pm :30							

Currency of Internal Place Inventory

Currency of Place: Considers properties from which a church or ministry operates, and other properties owned, or which can be accessed, by the church or ministry.

Instructions:

Gather the leaders of your church to do an inventory of internal places:

1. Using Table VII, list the internal places and locations (the church properties) to which your church or ministry has access in the first column. (If different rooms in the building are used for different purposes, list them separately.)
2. Write down the activities that took place in the last year in each location in the second column.
3. Categorize the activities according to the currencies for which they are exchanged.
   - Time
   - Gracious Leadership
   - Relationship
   - Truth
   - Wellness
   - Money
   - Other Blessings
4. As you work through this exercise, what do you notice and wonder about...
   ...where your strengths are?
   ...where your struggles are?
5. If you were to increase your community's or ministry's missional effort and sustainability:
   - What do you need to pay attention to?
   - In what ways can you refocus some of the existing activities to be exchanged for other currencies?
   - What new activities would you consider doing in order to develop further all the other currencies?
6. Develop a plan to further develop the currency of place for your church and the wider community in the coming year.

Table VII: Currency of Internal Place Inventory

Internal Locations	Activities	Currencies exchange: Gracious Leadership Relationship Truth Time and Place Money Wellness Other Blessings

Currency of External Place Inventory

Currency of Place: Refers to the properties from which a church and ministry operates, and other properties owned, or which can be accessed, by the church and ministry.

Instructions:

Gather the leaders of your church to do an inventory of external places:

1. Using Table VIII, list the external places and locations (other than the church properties) to which your church or ministry has access in the first column. For example, member's home, local businesses, public places, schools, etc.
2. Write down the activities that took place in the last year in each location in the second column.
3. Categorize the activities according to the currencies for which they are exchanged.
   - Time
   - Gracious Leadership
   - Relationship
   - Truth
   - Wellness
   - Money
4. As you work through this exercise, what do you notice and wonder about…
   - where your strengths are?
   - where your struggles are?
5. If you were to increase your community's or ministry's missional effort and sustainability:
   - What do you need to pay attention to?
   - In what ways can you refocus some of the existing activities to be exchanged for other currencies?
   - What new places in the wider community would you consider trying to gain access to? What ministry would you offer there?
6. Develop a plan to further develop the currency of place for your church and the wider community in the coming year.

Table VIII: Currency of External Place Inventory

External Locations	Activities	Currencies exchange: Gracious Leadership Relationship Truth Time and Place Money Wellness Other Blessings

Currency of Money Inventory

Currency of Money: "Money" here means something generally accepted as a medium of exchange, a measure of value, or as a means of payment.

Instructions:

1. Obtain a copy of your church and ministry budget.
2. Go through each expense item and categorize it according to the currencies that it is exchanged for: (Time, Place, Gracious Leadership, Relationship, Truth, or Wellness.)
3. Add up the amount of money for each currency exchange and write the amounts below:

    Time: _____

    Place: _____

    Gracious Leadership: _____

    Relationship: _____

    Truth: _____

    Wellness: _____

4. As you work through this exercise, what do you notice and wonder about...
   - what the strengths are?
   - what the struggles are?
5. If you were to increase your church's and ministry's sustainability:
   - What do you need to pay attention to?
   - What adjustment would you make in how you use your money?
6. Reconstruct a budget format that depicts how money is distributed in exchange for the other currencies in the Cycle of Blessings. What would next year's budget looks like?

Summary of Learning from Currency Inventory

Having worked through all the inventory exercises, answer the following questions to summarize your learning:

1. Which currencies are your strengths?
2. Which currencies are your weaknesses?

3. Do you have a balance of internal and external movements in the development and use of your currencies? Which currencies are out of balance?

4. What would you do in order to develop those currencies in which you are lacking?

5. If you were to increase your community's or ministry's missional effort and sustainability:
   - What do you need to pay attention to?
   - In what ways can you refocus some of the existing activities to develop and maximize the use of your currencies?

6. In what ways can you assist more leaders and members of your church to more fully understand the Cycle of Blessings and apply it to their lives and ministries?

7. Create a six-month action plan to move your church toward greater sustainability and becoming more missional.

Appendix B

How Are the Currencies Flowing in Your Ministry?

1. Make a list of ministries in which you are presently engaged.
2. Select one ministry of which you have the most knowledge: its mission, finances, organizing, populations served, etc.
3. Using the worksheet provided on page 171, in and around each one of the boxes representing one of the currencies that this ministry currently possesses write down as many items as you can think of. If you are working on this with others serving in the same ministry, feel free to have discussions with them.
4. Remembering that these currencies are of little value unless they are exchanged for blessings or other currencies, draw arrows representing how these currencies are currently flowing. For example, given the budget this ministry has (money), part of it goes to maintaining the building and the salary for the staff, so put an arrow from "money" to "time and place." If your ministry has a budget item for gracious-leadership training, then put an arrow from "money" to "gracious leadership." To give another example, a church currently has significant relationships with civic and community leaders by hosting a monthly community-wellness meeting in the church building. For this, put two arrows coming from "time and place": one going to "relationship," and the other going to "wellness."
5. As you work though this exercise, what do you notice and wonder about...
   * where the strengths of this ministry are?
   * where the weaknesses are?

If you were to maximize the Cycle of Blessings for this ministry, making it missional and sustainable:
   * What do you need to pay attention to?
   * In what ways can you refocus some of the existing activities?
   * What new activities would you consider doing?

6. Redesign a ministry plan for the coming year, incorporating all the currencies of the Cycle of Blessings:
   a. Name the truth you are seeking and the wellness you are fostering in this redesigned ministry;
   b. Construct a relational network that supports this ministry;
   c. Establish a place and time in which this ministry will take place;
   d. Create a wellness plan for people involved;
   e. Develop a leadership-training process to empower people for this ministry;
   f. Find investors to give money, time, and talent to relaunch this ministry;
   g. Formulate a financial plan for ongoing financial sustainability, perhaps using GracEconomics; and
   h. Project a time frame when this ministry will be self-sustaining.

How Are the Currencies Flowing in Your Ministry?

Gracious
Leadership

Time and Place

Relationship

Money

Truth

Wellness

Other Books by *Eric H. F. Law*

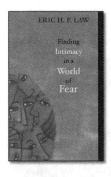

Finding Intimacy in a World of Fear

Finding Intimacy in a World of Fear was written in the context of 9/11 and Hurricane Katrina, events that fostered a climate of fear. Individuals may not understand nor know how to cope with their fears, but marketers, media, and politicians certainly understand how to take advantage of fear and use it to sell products, gain attention, and win election support. Law offers guidance through the landscape of fear and a path to follow and minister for Jesus in trust and intimacy.

• 9780827210417, $14.99

Inclusion

Making Room for Grace

Inclusion is the discipline of consciously extending the boundaries of our communities to embrace and affirm people of diverse backgrounds and experiences. In this resource for ministers and church leaders, Law provides models, theories, and strategies that are both practical and theologically sound for moving faith communities toward greater inclusion.

• 9780827216204, $16.99

The Wolf Shall Dwell with the Lamb

A Spirituality for Leadership in a Multicultural Community

This groundbreaking work explores how certain cultures consciously and unconsciously dominate in multicultural situations and what can be done about it.

• 9780827242319, $16.99

The Bush Was Blazing but Not Consumed

Building on the foundation set by *The Wolf Shall Dwell with the Lamb,* Law shows how to work with the dynamics of diverse cultures to create a truly inclusive community.

• 9780827202221, $16.99

CHALICE PRESS

For a complete listing and to learn more about the books listed above, visit **ChalicePress.com**

Additional Resources to Equip the Leaders of Your Church

SO MUCH BETTER

How Thousands of Pastors Help Each Other Thrive

by The Sustaining Pastoral Excellence Peer Learning Project
Penny Long Marler ■ D. Bruce Roberts ■ Janet Maykus ■ James Bowers
Larry Dill ■ Brenda K. Harewood ■ Richard Hester ■ Sheila Kirton-Robbins
Marianne LaBarre ■ Lis Van Harten ■ Kelli Walker-Jones

So Much Better demonstrates how peer-group participation gives pastors a critical jolt of energy and excitement—and how that translates into better ministry. Going beyond numbers and data, *So Much Better* shares stories and examples from participants, family, and church members who have seen the impact of peer groups firsthand.

• 9780827235243, $24.99

Leadership That Fits Your Church

What Kind of Pastor for What Kind of Congregation

by Cynthia Woolever & Deborah Bruce

Leadership That Fits Your Church explores how to find what really works for pastors and congregations. Cynthia Woolever and Deborah Bruce, known for their extensive work with congregational life research, lead you on an enlightening adventure in finding that perfect match.

• 9780827221734, $19.99

Leading Congregations through Crisis

by Gregory L. Hunt

Putting Christ and mission at the book's center, Hunt examines what happens when crisis strikes and how pastors and congregations can prepare for future events. Ten different types of crises — ranging from violence to natural disasters to internal congregational strife — provide insight into how pastors lead congregations through harrowing times into a healthy future.

• 9780827221703, $19.99

The Calling of Congregational Leadership

Being, Knowing, and Doing Ministry

by Larry L. McSwain

McSwain shows church leaders how to create communities that are vital and reflective of God's mission in the world.

• 9780827205314, $24.99

TheColumbiaPartnership.org   ChalicePress.com • 1-800-366-3383

All titles listed above are part of *The Columbia Partnership Leadership Series*